Date Due

27148

6/HELEN
+ICDN

GABBY, ERNIE AND ME

GABBY, ERNIE AND ME

A VANCOUVER BOYHOOD

— • • • —

TED ASHLEE

— • • • —

J.J. DOUGLAS
VANCOUVER

J.J. Douglas Ltd.
1875 Welch Street
North Vancouver, British Columbia

                            .

Ashlee, Ted, 1914-
    Gabby, Ernie, and me

    Canadian Cataloguing in Publicaton Data

    Ashlee, Ted, 1914—
        Gabby, Ernie, and me

        ISBN 0-88894-059-9

        1. Ashlee, Ted, 1914—   I. Title.
    FC3847.4.A849   971.1'33   C76-016070-8
    F1089.5.V22A

    Library of Congress catalog card number
    76-48401

Design and production co-ordination by Mike Yazzolino
Typeset by Domino-Link Word and Data Processing
Printed and bound in Canada by The Hunter Rose Company

CONTENTS

To **Gabby,**
James Brownlea Geddes

To **Ernie,**
Ernest Lothian Gaston

To **Swede,**
Walter Sorensen

To **Torchy,**
the late Donald MacPherson Geddes

TUGBOAT
ROUND
THE
BEND

*J*ust after sunset on a fine summer evening, as automobiles streamed bumper to bumper from Lansdowne Park Race Track to the Marpole bridge, a tug down river hooted imperiously. Van Courtland, the bridge tender, halted the traffic flow. Ancient machinery clanked into protesting motion and the bridge span creaked open. Van Courtland studied the slowly approaching ship. She appeared to be a big one, judging from the height of her red and green running lights. On her tall mast three white lights, indicating a tow of more than a cable's length astern, shone brightly in the gathering gloom. Van Courtland waited. The cars waited, three miles of them.

About a month previously Ernie had spoken at length on the psychological effect that the ability to wield unchallenged power had on some people. He mentioned Caesar and Ghengis Khan. Closer to home, he felt, was such a simple act as taking a boat up the Fraser River or out of False Creek. A bridge had to be opened. People had to wait, respectfully, as the ship passed through. The man in charge had his moment of glory, his opportunity to know the thrill of unquestioned authority. It made sense.

Accordingly, we set about building a ship. We scrounged an old seineboat skiff and worked hard fitting a new bottom plank. We caulked the seams with scrap rope and poured tar into the cracks. A tall young hemlock was dragged out of the woods near Garfey's Pond and denuded of limbs and bark. It made a fine mast with all the stays and braces rigged in a proper seamanlike fashion. A high outrigger arrangement made of two-by-threes provided a base for her running lights.

At this point we called for help. Gabby's brother Torchy, a scientific type, hooked up a collection of dry cell batteries to provide the necessary voltage for the lights, which were six-volt automotive bulbs inside peanut butter jars. The red and green for the running lights were created by the simple expedient of wrapping these jars in coloured cellophane.

The whistle proved a real problem. Ernie managed to scrounge one somewhere, a battered brass affair, which Gabby overhauled and polished bright as a salmon lure. My job was to provide an air tank. That wasn't easy, but I finally conned a local garage man into lending me a compressed air cylinder belonging to his acetylene welder. This, along with plumbing fittings fastened together in a manner which would have sent a steam fitter running for cover, provided power for our whistle.

When our ship had been launched with due ceremony, we were horrified to discover that the mast and outrigger made her dangerously top heavy. This was corrected by the addition of several hundred pounds of stones. As ballast they worked fine, but the resulting pressure caused a number of not too serious leaks.

After waiting for what we considered to be the right time, we rowed out of our hidden harbour on Jimmie's Island and bore down on the Marpole bridge. Gabby and I pulled on the long oars. Ernie handled the tiller with one hand and clutched the whistle cord with the other. Fifty yards from the bridge Ernie sounded three blasts. The bridge opened. Van Courtland waited.

Gabby and I strained at the sweeps. We might have been rowing in a river of glue for all the headway we made. Then it hit us. The tide had turned, and in the grip of the ebb current we were helpless.

Half an hour of waiting and three or four miles of honking cars finally unnerved the bridge tender. He turned on his powerful searchlight. He and everyone else could see us plainly: two lanky teenagers, working like galley slaves. Ernie blew the whistle, derisively.

Van Courtland's roars of rage were all but drowned in the spectators' laughter, and we had lost all hope of knowing the thrill of exercising unchallenged authority.

THE
HERMIT
OF
DRIFTWOOD
COVE

A few miles northwest of Pender Harbour near Vancouver lies an island of some two thousand acres thickly forested with Douglas fir and red cedar. At the southern end of the island there is a deep bay wide open to the winter sou'easters. The wind, helped by a tidal eddy, seems to collect most of the driftwood in the Strait of Georgia and then pile it onto the beach. With brilliant originality, the local citizens call it Driftwood Cove although no such name appears on mariners' charts.

Gabby, Ernie, and I, the inseparable three, explored Driftwood Cove one summer vacation. We beached our rowboat, clambered over a mountain of logs, stumps, rotted wharf planks and assorted jetsam of the deep, and discovered a tidy clearing in the wood. In front of a cabin built of logs, cedar shakes, and stone an ancient, bearded man sat in his rocking chair, soaking up sunshine and chuckling to himself.

We approached cautiously, not knowing what kind of reception to expect. The old man greeted us cheerfully.

"Mornin' boys," he said. "I was getting just a mite lonely, not having talked to anybody since the police was here last fall. I hear the kettle boilin'. One of you nip into the cabin and make tea."

Gabby and Ernie hung back, so I reluctantly entered the cottage. The interior was surprisingly clean and well organized. I made tea and carried out the big enamelled iron pot and four mugs on a tray fashioned from a cedar shake. The tea was strong and hot. We sipped carefully and without much enthusiasm, since we were unaccustomed to tea devoid of cream and sugar. The old gentleman held his mug an inch from his scraggy moustache and consumed the scalding liquid with a melodious application of the vacuum principle.

"Well, now, boys,"said our host, setting his cup down on the chopping block, "I gather from listening to you that the solemn looking guy is Gabby, curly-head is Ernie and the long-geared one is Ted. Just call me Hermit like everybody does. Come out back and I'll show you my deer."

There were no deer in the field behind the house. Then the hermit whistled and a half dozen does and two bucks with velvet antlers bounded out of the woods. The old man tossed them a few carrots.

"Beautiful, ain't they? Come with me and I'll show you around my property."

We followed a trail through the cool, richly scented forest, stopping frequently to admire a particularly lush growth of sword fern, a bear-biscuit fungus half the size of a kitchen table, and a blackened stump that looked vaguely like a standing bear. Ernie, leading our party, suddenly let out a yelp of fear and amazement. We dashed up to where he stood pointing a shaking finger at a grisly discovery half hidden in the bracken—ribs and other bones, some rotting clothing and the rusting remains of a Winchester carbine.

"Hold on a minute," said the old hermit as we turned to run. "There's a story you've got to hear. Sit down on that log and listen to me.

"Last fall, it was," said the old gent, "around the beginning of October. A cabin cruiser anchored in my cove and some young fellers come ashore. There was four of them. Well, I was glad to have company so I gave them tea and whistled up my deer. I could see by the way they looked at each other that they figured on coming back for a hunting trip. I showed them my land and led them along this trail to make sure that they found the skeleton. 'What happened?' says one of the young fellers.

" 'Oh,' says I, casual like, 'sometimes a hunter comes here to shoot my deer. I've got an answer for him, all right!' Well, they

7

left in such a hurry their coat tails was fair snapping. Next day two game wardens arrived. I played innocent and when we come to the skeleton the young cop grabbed me with one hand and hauled out his handcuffs with the other. The older police-man looked at the bones and laughed fit to bust.

" 'Let him go, Charlie,' he says to the young cop. 'These are deer bones. That's a neat trick, old timer. In your own way you are a real conservationist. Your secret is safe with us. We will tell the people who reported this that you can be dangerous and should be left alone. How long have you had this scene rigged up?'

" 'Four year,' I tells the game warden. 'One fall a feller wounded one of my deer and left it to die. I found the skeleton in the spring and used some of its bones, my old clothes and a worn-out rifle to set it up. Artistic, ain't it!' "

We walked back to the cabin, and the old hermit made a request.

"You won't tell anybody, will you boys?" he asked. "I think that was the best joke anybody ever figured out, and my deer is safe. I been laughing about it ever since I put the run on them young fellers. You heard me laughing when you got here."

We promised to keep his secret. Now that the hermit has been dead and gone for years and his cabin replaced by a fine summer home, his story can be told.

8

HAPPINESS
IS A
RAINED
OUT
PICNIC

*O*f all the curses visited upon mankind nothing, not the Bomb, not famine, pestilence or war, can compare with the horrors inflicted by the Large Group Picnic. A small picnic is all right, one involving a family or a selection of intimate friends or a small group of kids on an outing. Great. Marvellous. A get-together at some uncrowded beach or beside a mountain stream or on any old rundown farm can be pure pleasure. But to become involved in a large, disorganized, panicky picnic is an experience to try the soul.

When I was a kid my aunts were inveterate picnickers. To give them credit, their plans always began sensibly enough but invariably got out of hand. They would reach a decision. We, just the family and a couple of my friends, would go to Second Beach, English Bay or Stanley Park to swim, listen to the band or just loaf around and eat. Then the word would get out somehow, and messages from other families and friends would be carried by telephone, runners, smoke signals or some mysterious form of communication until forty or fifty people had invited themselves, and our modest outing was transformed into a social disaster. As the scarred veteran of many such forays, let me recount one of them. It ran true to form.

The O'Malleys were the first to muscle in, all eleven of them, including that seven-year-old horror, Michael. Michael's favourite diversion was to walk up to anyone, even a stranger, look up at him innocently, deliver a shin-peeling kick and run screeching to his mother, his victim in hostile pursuit intending, rightly so, to wring the little perisher's neck. The O'Malleys ran to height, and there was about five foot eleven of Mrs. O'Malley, topped off by a fierce Irish mug and the shoulders of a longshoreman.

"And what have you done to me darlin' boy?" she would

demand. "Chasin' him like a murderer, so ye are. Begone now, before I break this chair across yere back."

The victim always retreated hastily.

So the O'Malleys arrived at our house, in good time as was their custom , along with seven Robinsons, the entire Malchewski family, including their five cousins recently arrived from Saskatchewan, and others too numerous and too horrific to enumerate. Gabby, Ernie, and I cringed in a corner, unnoticed in the turmoil, expecting the worst.

At that time no one in our immediate circle owned an automobile, so we all trooped down to the interurban tram and crowded on, completely filling one coach with ourselves, our picnic baskets, unbelievable noise, and young shin-kicking Michael, who seemed to be everywhere. It was clear to us three inseparables that we would have been much better off elsewhere.

It was necessary to transfer to the Davie Street tramcar to complete the journey to English Bay, and that was where the real trouble began. Ernie led the exodus from the interurban at Davie Street, struggling with two vast sandwich-filled suitcases and clenching his streetcar transfer between his teeth. As he raced around behind the tram, a suitcase lid flew open, sandwiches carpeted the road, and instantly every stray dog in Vancouver converged upon them with joyous yelps. Ernie tried valiantly to fight off dogs with one hand and retrieve foodstuffs with the other. Mrs. O'Malley kicked a path through the thieving curs, and everyone descended upon the waiting tram. Then Ernie discovered that he had lost his transfer. The conductor was demanding another fare from the embarrassed youngster when Mrs. O'Malley caught his eye.

"Pass, friend," he said.

Our mob—there is no other word for it—thundered into the

picnic area and took over. There was a huge public cook stove, fashioned of firebrick with a rusty steel top, into which the men crammed enough wood to fire a steam donkey boiler. They lit it and in minutes the steel plate glowed red even in the bright summer sun. The cooks—Mesdames O'Malley, Robinson, and Malchewski—could not get near it, and fell to berating their willing helpers in voices reminiscent of a Sioux war party attacking the Seventh Cavalry.

At that moment Moira O'Malley, aged twelve, announced hysterically that Michael was lost.

All activity ceased instantly and Mr. Robinson, late of the Coldstream Guards and wearing a waxed moustache to prove it, came to attention, gave his moustache a twirl and barked orders.

"Search party, fall in. You, Malchewski, take party of eight, search wooded area due north. O'Malley, organize your family and scour wooded area west, keeping one arm's length apart."

And so it went, until everyone had been designated an area of reconnaissance. Except we three. Regimental Sergeant Major Robinson looked us over and was not too impressed with what he saw.

"You, long 'un," he addressed me, "take your chums and search rocky area along beach."

We clambered among the boulders bordering the sandy shore until Gabby discovered a natural fortress that was invisible to all passers-by.

"This will do," he said, producing packets of sandwiches and three bottles of pop from his jacket pockets. "Relax, everybody."

What of Michael, we wanted to know? Much as we loathed the little beast, should not our search continue?

"No need," said Gabby. "He's up in that big maple by the cook stove . I saw him there, laughing at us. Have a sandwich."

We had our lunch, drank pop, spent a leisurely hour strolling along the beach collecting sea shells and skipping stones, then wandered back to the picnic site to discover that Michael had been found and that R.S.M. Robinson had organized a party to search for us.

Everyone got together eventually, and we commandeered six of the best tables, all shaded by giant maples and cedars, upon which the women had set out enough food to supply us and all the neighbouring picnickers as well.

Splat. A large raindrop plunked into Mrs. O'Malley's cup of tea. And another. And another. Our oceanic climate, ever unpredictable, had produced a summer rainstorm.

In the pandemonium that followed, most of the refreshments became a sodden ruin before they could be packed away. A few articles—a teapot, several dishes and a number of swimsuits —were abandoned in the wild rush for the streetcar waiting six blocks away. We made it, finally, wringing wet but surprisingly cheerful, all things considered.

We three, standing in the vestibule as usual, watched the rain streaming down the windows and were cheered by the thought that luck for once had been on our side. Usually we struggled home after sunset, bone weary, with that bilious feeling one gets when on the edge of heat prostration. This was much better. Good old rain had terminated our sufferings.

RUN,
CRAB,
RUN

*A*nyone watching us, wet, weary and dirty, toiling along Oak Street on that hot Saturday afternoon, would wonder how four growing boys could get into such a mess. For us it was easy. We had been ordered off the number seventeen Oak Street car, thirty-four blocks before our destination, and told in stentorian tones never again to darken the doors of that ancient and worthy streetcar. All because of a harmless prank.

We had spent the morning, Gabby, Ernie, and I and a tall towhead called Swede, down at the Gore Avenue wharf fishing for crabs. Our equipment was simple. Our method was even simpler, but called for precise timing and flawless co-operation. We would tie a chunk of raw beef to the end of a heavy handline and lower it to the bottom. When a crab took hold of the bait, we slowly and carefully pulled it to the top. Just as the prize reached the surface one of us would ease a plank under it, and, with a dexterous upward thrust, flip the crab onto the float. Sometimes. Usually the intended victim slithered off the board and escaped. We stuck at it, however, catching a few, losing many, and soaking each other every time the plank shot out of the water. Eventually, we filled a potato sack with clicking, claw-snapping crustaceans and started for home.

This meant a long, long hike to the tram line and a transfer onto number seventeen at Cambie and Hastings. As the car was filled to capacity with housewives loaded down with their week's shopping, we moved to the vestibule at the rear to stand with a number of labourers who had knocked off work at noon.

After a time it occurred to us that it might be fun to stage a crab race. We gingerly lifted a dozen brawny specimens from the sack, and we and the labourers each selected a likely-looking candidate.

One seemed to have special appeal. Broad-shelled, barnacle-encrusted and mean-looking, he inspired some of the more affluent punters to bet as high as a dime on his potential speed. Having no confidence in muscle men in track and field, I chose a lean-limbed, racy-looking youngster, a Sea Biscuit of the undersea set, and put my all, five cents, on what had to be a winner.

We lined up our field, someone yelled "Go," and they took off full tilt, urged on by shouts of encouragement from the gallery. As the crabs dashed into the car with their erratic sideways gait, one of the women spotted the approaching horde. Her terrified shriek nearly lifted the roof off old number seventeen. Other women joined in, and soon all the shoppers were standing on the seats, screaming. All except the two who had fainted.

Harry, the motorman, jammed on the brakes. Women, parcels, crabs, and punters hurtled forward in a mass of groping limbs, crushed parcels and smashed eggs. Harry, on the verge of hysteria, shouted commands. His sergeant major's voice finally took effect. Housewives untangled themselves, but continued to scream, pointing at us the while. Harry demanded that we explain our behaviour. We tried, but somehow the logic of our experiment eluded him. We learned one lesson: the impossibility of attempting to argue with a sergeant major, even one who had been home from the Great War for several years.

So the motorman, shaking with rage, ordered us to collect every so-and-so crab, get them back into the such-and-such sack, and remove it and ourselves from his streetcar. Promptly! Now!

The task was not easy: we had to crawl around under the seats in a mess of squashed vegetables and broken eggs, reaching into hiding places where crabs might be—and were—poised with claws ready to nip our groping fingers. Painfully. Finally we captured them, and lugging the heavy sack, trooped through the door, followed by caustic jibes from the passengers.

So we struggled along in the summer heat, taking turns with the sack to divide the labour—and the discomfort of having the sack drip onto our trousers a malodorous mixture of stale potato-flavoured harbour water and the body liquid of expiring crabs.

We had assured Harry, in all sincerity, that we had captured every crab, but a re-count proved us wrong. My long-legged racer was missing. We never did find out what happened to that one.

JOHN
PATRICK
AND
THE
LEPRECHAUN

*H*e was born in County Meath, where the best cattle and the most potent poteen in all Ireland are to be found. All his life he carried a shillelagh—a seasoned bit of blackthorn root, so it was, from Rory's bog. A small man was he, blue-eyed, sinewy, Irish as the pigs of Drogheda. He was John Patrick Ryan, my maternal grandfather.

Let other lands have their Paul Bunyans, Sam Smalls and Tyl Euilanspiegels. Grandfather told us tales of the greatest of all folk heroes, that crafty trio, Hadden and Dadden and Dan O'Neil. He was on familiar terms with the "little people," as he called the leprechauns, and knew full well the portent of evil when will-o'-the-wisps danced wraith-like across the bogs.

John Patrick even claimed an acquaintanceship with Finn McCool, the blacksmith of Slane who was the strongest man that ever lived.

"I'm tellin' the truth now, boys," Grandfather would tell us. "Finn McCool would climb a ladder with a barrel of ale balanced on either hand and then calmly climb down again. He would test a newly sharpened plow by pulling it through the tough Meath sod making a neat furrow, so he would. Then, to prove that he felt no fatigue, the darlin' man would pick himself up by the nape of the neck and hold himself out at arm's length."

The story we enjoyed most concerned Grandfather's escape, as he called it, from the poverty of Ireland to a business of his own in the relative affluence of British Columbia. Seated on tool boxes in his little plumber's shop, watching him cut and thread iron pipe, we would listen to his tale told in a brogue thick as clotted cream.

"I tell ye, me buckos," he would say, "life in the south was a chancey thing. There were Finnigan's Raiders and O'Donnell's Bog Boys and other private armies, ill organized as they were, forever making war on the English landlords. The English landowners were away most of the time, so the worst they suffered was the occasional burned-down barn or cattle theft. The fights always ended up with Irishmen killing Irishmen, and an awful thing it was."

"The best plan, it seemed to me, was to clear out of Meath altogether," Grandfather would continue as he squirted oil on his thread cutter. "With the endless stone-throwing and creeping through the mists on useless raids, business was at a standstill, and even a fine tradesman like meself was unemployed most of the time. I collected my tools and wearing all the clothing I owned I travelled by night to the Irish Sea, where I begged a lift on a fishing smack. We sailed across St. George's Channel and at dawn the fishermen rowed me ashore and left me on the beach near Llandudno in North Wales. After many days of walking and riding in farm wagons I arrived in London in grand style in a brewer's dray. I worked in London for two years and saved enough money to buy a steerage ticket on an immigrant ship headed for Montreal. I worked my way across this vast land where people were friendly toward me and any distance under a thousand miles wasn't worth mentioning."

So when we were eight or nine years old, Gabby, Ernie, and I—faced with a mystery beyond the penetration of our young minds—turned to an authority with the wisdom of age and the ancients.

We three had spent a Saturday fishing for chub along the Fraser River sand bars, clambering over log booms—a forbidden activity—and searching the wild rose thickets for birds' nests. On all fours through a thorny tunnel we followed the tracks of a muskrat, clearly imprinted in the damp clay. We suddenly realized that the animal tracks had been obliterated at regular intervals by small footprints: not of bare feet, not of sturdy boots such as ours, but of something which resembled slightly pointed mocassins. It occurred to us that a small child had wandered off in his bedroom slippers and was lost. The nearest house was a good half mile away. Worried, we traced the tiny footprints to the edge of a water-filled ditch. There the trail ended. Sick with apprehension, we considered searching the water for a drowned child, but decided instead to cross the flats to that lone house and call the police. Then Gabby noticed that the footprints reappeared on the other side of the ditch. I jumped across first, no easy task even for my long legs, and caught the others as they flailed over, landing off balance. How could a three- or four-year old—and no one larger could have walked upright through the wild rose tunnel—have made such a leap? More fearful than we would admit, we traced the footprints along a trail winding through the coarse swamp grass.

The river flat ended at a steep bank forested in alder and maple, and although the trail continued, our small walker had left no marks on the packed earth. Admitting defeat, we hiked home to consult Grandfather.

"Well, now," he said when he had heard the breathless account of our adventure, "if we were in Meath the explanation would be simple enough. You would have been following a leprechaun, so you would. Not a banshee, which would have set up such a howl at your intrusion that the hair on your scalps would have stood on end. But what is one of the Little People doin' so far from the Old Sod? You must take me to your river flats tomorrow. I shall attend early Mass, and if you young heathens can occupy yourselves without mischief until my return, all well and good. Why am I threatening you? You know that we will go in any case."

22

The old man wandered away and we could hear him muttering, "A leprechaun here? Impossible. Unless I unwittingly brought one over with me in my trunk. Or hidden beneath my pipe tobacco in my bog oak humidor. Aye, that's it. The magic of bog oak is well known."

Knowing that Grandfather could not easily crawl through the wild rose tunnel or leap the ditch, we started our search where the small one had entered the flats. The tracks were still there, faint but visible. We followed them to the tree-covered bank, and from there John Patrick took command.

"Scatter yourselves," he ordered, "and look for fairy rings. You don't know what they are? I'm ashamed that the grandson of an Irishman should not know that. A fairy ring is a circle of toadstools and will be hard to find. Watch for a small clearing among the sword ferns. If you find a fairy ring, don't touch it. Call me."

Ernie found it: a circle of toadstools four feet in diameter with a very large one in the centre.

"So," said Grandfather. "A meeting place, so it is. The chieftain sits on the toadstool in the middle like a chairman at any meeting. He makes all final decisions and the others obey orders. Move away carefully, now. No doubt we are being watched."

With the old man leading, we returned to the forest path. Halfway to the river we met a rough-looking man carrying a .22 rifle. He was crouching low and studying the tracks we had followed.

"I'm tracking a raccoon," he said, friendly enough. "Did you kids see one in the woods, yonder?"

"Since when, me bucko," said Grandfather, "does a raccoon walk on its hind legs and wear shoes?"

"Shoes?" the man asked. "Are you crazy? No, I see you're not.

I apologize. But you are not a woodsman, or you would know that the clay was not wet enough for the 'coon's front paws to leave a mark, and his hind feet left only blurred tracks. Come to think of it, they do look like small feet in pointed shoes."

The man with the rifle left to carry on with his tracking. As soon as he was out of earshot John Patrick set our minds at ease.

"The dear man is right about one thing," he said. "I'm no woodsman, I confess. I'm an Irish plumber, but like all Irishmen I can recognize a leprechaun's footprints when I see them. Moreover, the man will never see the Little People, woodsman though he is. If he disturbs them with his tramping through the ferns he will find himself tripping over unseen things, and perhaps hear the banshee's wailing laughter. What a grand thought that is. Come along, me buckos, we must be home by teatime."

The woodsman could have been right, of course, but we preferred to believe Grandfather. After all, the man was a stranger. John Patrick was one of us.

TROUBLE,
TROUBLE

*T*hinking back over the aeons since my youth it surprises me how we, and others, managed to get into so much trouble by merely travelling on the old Oak Street tram. Even Harry the motorman knew moments of terror, and once felt the hot breath of the law scorching his guileless neck.

One Saturday morning we were heading downtown, Harry having forgiven us for the crab racing episode, when a passenger began complaining bitterly about the pheasants scratching up his garden. According to him, pheasants in a garden constituted an infinitely greater menace than the most ravenous domestic hens. His newly seeded lawn was a mess, his green pea patch a disaster area.

Everyone made helpful suggestions, from scarecrows to twelve-gauge shotguns. It was Harry, as usual, who offered the most logical solution.

"In the Old Country," he said, in modified parade square tones, "we had the same problem. Since we were not allowed firearms—only the gentry were allowed to shoot, you understand—we resorted to trapping. Using a trap something like the kind used in this country for gophers, we covered the bait pan with tar and stuck white dried peas on it. We would scatter a few around the garden. The pheasant would eat some of them, but sooner or later he would peck at the peas in the trap. Wham! Broken neck. Pheasant for dinner."

Logical.

On that particular Saturday, our journey downtown was for a treat that occurred too seldom in our young lives. Each of us had been given carfare and fifty cents to spend. That meant a thirty-cent restaurant meal and a matinee at one of the less salubrious Hastings Street movie houses which included a Hoot Gibson western and episode 118 of *Tarzan and the Apes* for fifteen cents. That left a nickel for a bag of popcorn.

Stuffed with popcorn and hoarse from alternatively hissing the villain and cheering Hoot Gibson's valiant rescue of the damsel with too much eye makeup, we boarded number seventeen at Cambie Street and proceeded, as was our custom, to the less crowded vestibule at the rear.

We studied our fellow passengers. There were a couple of labourers, three B.C. Electric motormen, and a conductor whom we knew to be a first-class magician who often entertained at house parties, club luncheons, and the like. Also present was an elderly Chinese market gardener with an enormous sack of cabbages.

At 25th Avenue or thereabouts, the magician reached over to the sack and selected a cabbage. He examined it carefully, made a slit with his pocketknife, and extracted a fifty-cent piece, which he dropped into his vest pocket. Nobody said anything. The Chinese gardener regarded him solemnly.

The magician selected another cabbage from which he extracted another four bits. And another. We heard the coins clink as he dropped them into his pocket. Then he leaned back against the wall. Nobody spoke.

Number seventeen lurched along her wavy track oblivious of impending disaster. The Chinese gardener, keeping his balance with difficulty in the swaying coach, produced a long pastry knife from the inner recesses of his tattered coat. With one swipe he dissected a cabbage. Since no money was forthcoming he tried again. Another cabbage was fished out of the sack. He chopped that one to bits. By the time we reached Marpole the sack was empty, the floor ankle deep in coleslaw, and the unfortunate gardener yelling hysterically in Cantonese.

A week later we were on our way downtown once more—but simply to window shop the sporting goods stores, since we possessed only carfare. The passenger who had complained about the pheasants climbed aboard looking cheerful.

"Hey, Harry," he sang out, "I did like you said, Harry. I set a bunch of gopher traps with dried peas glued on 'em and, boy, was I lucky. Caught three cock birds and a hen. Can I give you one?"

Standing nearby was a big man in khaki. There was a revolver on his hip and a green stripe along the outside seam of his trousers. His brass buttons gleamed menacingly.

"What's all this about pheasant trapping? I'm Atkins, the game warden. You caught four, you say? What's your name?"

YON'S
NO A
HAMMER,
MacSNIRTLE

*I*n the years preceding World War I and for a long time after, the majority of the Vancouver police were Highland Scots. Most of them were big, easygoing, and reasonably honest, although some who possessed none of these qualities unfortunately rose to high rank on the force and were frequently "busted" following investigations by the police commission.

This is a story about two policemen who represented opposite ends of the scale. One was Big Sandy, six feet five and dear knows how heavy, who had once been champion caber tosser of all Scotland. The other was Angus MacSnirtle, powerful, bad tempered, crafty and disliked by all in general and Big Sandy in particular.

MacSnirtle was a hammer thrower. After his return from the 1920 Olympic Games in Antwerp he carried on with his sport, appearing year after year at the Caledonian Games, where he usually won top honours. Angus worked his way up through the ranks of the police force to one of the top positions and was finally expelled for a series of misdemeanours too numerous to mention here.

Big Sandy was incapable of even the mildest forms of skulduggery and was beloved by all, especially the children.

At the time of this story, about 1924 or '25, traffic lights had not appeared on the Vancouver scene and vehicles were directed by a police constable on point duty. A young recruit had to work up to that position, and part of his training was to escort school children across the busier streets. Big Sandy was particularly good at this. Knee deep in Grade One'ers, matching his great stride to their little legs, Sandy would solemnly herd his small charges across the street—and woe betide anyone who so much as looked unfriendly toward them. On occasions when a motorist failed to stop quickly enough to suit him, Sandy would give the signal to halt, and the hand that made it was the size of a grain scoop.

"Ah'm watchin' ye," he would roar.

Unlike MacSnirtle, Sandy would good-naturedly put up with all manner of ribbing, provided it was in the spirit of good, clean fun. On the corner of Granville and Hastings, my father—who was an Englishman and could therefore never overlook an opportunity to give a Scot a bad time—once explained, much to Sandy's delight, how Highlanders were recruited for the Vancouver Police Force.

According to Pop, when the local constabulary needed bolstering up, a representative from the police commission journeyed to the north of Scotland. He placed bear traps, baited with haggis, at strategic spots among the heather where wild Highlanders were known to lurk. When several of the big brutes had been captured, they were half tamed, taught the rudiments of the English language, and shipped to Vancouver.

"Roll up your sleeve, Sandy," said Pop, "and show us where the trap caught you."

Grinning broadly, Big Sandy, with some difficulty, worked his tunic sleeve over a forearm thick as a truck tire. Sure enough, there was a scar. Even Pop was taken aback.

One Saturday afternoon Gabby, Ernie, and I were watching Angus MacSnirtle, dressed in kilt and singlet, train for the next Caledonian Games. He would grasp the handle attached to the steel cable, glare at us, whirl around and around until the hammer was fairly whistling, and let fly, throwing the missile an unbelievable distance. Much as we loathed the man we had to admire his style. Then Big Sandy arrived.

"What d'ye think ye're doin', ma wee mannie?" he asked, wearing an expression that was awfully close to a sneer.

"Ah'm throwin' a hammer, that's what Ah'm doin'," replied

MacSnirtle, very irate, "as e'en a great, witless, gowk lik' yoursel' can plainly see."

"Aye, MacSnirtle," Sandy countered, "but wi' yere usual mush-headedness ye've aye owerlooked an important fact. Yon's no a hammer ye're wastin' yere time flingin' aboot. Yon's a wee iron ball wi' a wee bit string tied tae it. If ye're goin' tae throw a hammer then throw a real hammer as Ah would mysel'. Act lik' a mon, MacSnirtle."

His features liver-coloured with rage, the hammer thrower advanced and shook a large fist.

"Vurra weel, ye caber-tossin' oaf," he shouted, "Ah'll no gi' ye the clout ye richly deserve. Instead, Ah'll wager ye a day's salary that Ah can throw ma hammer at least twice as far as ye can throw an ordinara sledge anytime ye wish tae hae the contest."

"Ah, weel, MacSnirtle," Big Sandy sighed, producing a fourteen-pound blacksmith's maul from behind his back, "Ye asked for it, and made a wager before witnesses."

The giant struggled out of his tunic and shirt and handed them to Gabby. He twirled his sledge as if it were a tack hammer.

"You first, MacSnirtle," he said.

The brawny Scot whirled his hammer with practised ease and let go over his shoulder, as was the custom. It was a fine throw.

Sandy took his position and measured MacSnirtle's throw with an accurate eye.

"No bad," he said. "No bad."

Grasping his hammer handle in his huge hands, Big Sandy spun around and around with surprising speed and grace for so large a man, and threw with all his might. The maul soared aloft and seemed to hang in space as if preparing to go into orbit. Then it came down in a long curve and thudded into the ground a good three feet beyond MacSnirtle's mark.

No one spoke as Big Sandy shrugged into his shirt and tunic. We did not dare say anything, and Angus MacSnirtle was beyond speech.

"Will you laddies oblige me by returnin' yon hammer tae the blacksmith?" asked our Sandy.

We nodded. "Oh, aye, MacSnirtle," Big Sandy said as he turned to walk away at the regulation pace of two miles an hour, "Ah'll be watchin' for ye on payday, so dinnae attempt tae worm oot o' yere fullish wager."

THAT'S
SHOW
BIZ

*M*y father was very upset about the violence displayed in motion pictures. We three had just charged into the house after seeing Douglas Fairbanks in *The Sea Wolf*. Tremendously excited, and all talking at once, we explained how Doug Fairbanks, with a single bolt from his trusty crossbow, had picked off one of the bad guys, away up on the highest yardarm on the foremast. The bad guy, caught as he was about to hurl a knife at the Sea Wolf, fell in a dramatic parabola and splashed into the sea.

"Shocking," said Father, "quite shocking," and repaired to his study to write a scathing letter to the theatre manager.

The Sea Wolf was quite a movie, and Douglas Fairbanks was quite a man. Not much of an actor by today's standards, perhaps, but Fairbanks was an outstanding gymnast whose feats of skill and strength have never been approached, much less equalled, by any other actor, including the several Tarzans. He was great at rope climbing and one-arm chinups. He could leap tremendous distances with ease. Moreover, he performed all the daring deeds himself, refusing ever to use a stunt man.

As the Sea Wolf, Doug Fairbanks set out to capture a three-masted, square-rigged pirate ship. He swam out to the vessel swiftly, powerfully, with a dagger clenched in his teeth. He climbed onto the rudder, cut one rudder line, hauled the rudder over hard astarboard, and secured it so that the helmsman was unable to steer and the ship sailed helplessly in slow circles.

Fairbanks's next feat was to destroy the sails. He scrambled over the ship's transom and vaulted the rail, instantly engaging the cutlass-wielding crew in mortal combat. The slaughter was terrific. Hacking a path through the enemy, the Sea Wolf raced along the deck. He paused briefly to pick off the afore-mentioned bad guy, and then climbed up the mast to the fore t'gans'l yardarm. What happened next is unique in movie-making history and must have been Fairbanks's own idea. He stabbed his dagger through the sail and slid down it, gripping his knife hilt, thus neatly cutting the sail from top to bottom. Between brisk fights with the now demoralized crew, he repeated the operation on the rest of the sails.

I read later in a movie magazine that Fairbanks had come close to killing himself during the rehearsal of this episode. At his first attempt, his dagger was far too sharp. He slid down the canvas at a fearful rate, suffering first degree burns to one hand and forearm and hitting the deck with an awful wallop. Only his superb physical condition saved him from severe injury.

Those were the days, my friends. We took our movies seriously. They were silent movies, of course, with subtitles. In the smaller motion picture houses sound effects were produced by a pianist. Large downtown theatres had organists, and marvellous musicians they were. They could imitate cannon fire, a horse's whinny, or the crash of falling crockery. Those old-time organists could play anything, and their timing was always perfect.

However, we three inseparables preferred the neighbour-hood movie house. We could walk to it, and as an added attraction the price of admission was low. Patrons twelve years old or under paid five cents for Saturday matinees and ten cents in the evening. Those over twelve paid fifteen cents. Gabby and Ernie got away with a dime until they were fourteen and their voices broke. Being tall for my age, I was not so lucky. In fact I had several arguments with the ticket seller.

We enjoyed Saturday night movies more than any others. Quite apart from thrillers starring Tom Mix, Hoot Gibson,

William Farnham and other cowboy heroes there was always live entertainment supplied by local artists. They came on stage and performed for half an hour between the newsreel and the feature film. They sang, danced or delivered monologues. We also had some good jugglers, and there were two or three very bad ventriloquists.

One Saturday night a chap appeared on stage wearing a tweed jacket and a sporran over half a pair of trousers and half a kilt.

"I'm only half Scotch," he explained.

He carried a beribboned three-legged milking stool upside down to represent a bagpipe, and got a standing ovation for his cheerful rendition of "I'm the Only Yiddisher Scotchman in the Irish Fusileers."

Actually, his name was Mike O'Sullivan and he would do anything for a laugh. He had a fine voice and excellent diction. When he pranced about twirling a shillelagh and singing "One-Eyed Reilly" or "Clancy Lowered the Boom" in his rich brogue, we caught every word. In an abrupt change of mood Mike would sing sentimental Irish ballads that brought cheers from his audience and nostalgic sobs from the O'Malleys, the Murphys and the McDonnells seated in the front row.

On another Saturday evening a musical duo gave a memorable recital. One performer was tall and skinny with an arty mop of grey hair, a string tie, and a cutaway coat. His striped trousers appeared to have been used as a wind sock at a weather station. He carried a flute.

His partner was short, stout and pink: pink complexion, pink scalp, pink hair. His shirt, too, was pink, but in splotches, as if it had been washed along with red flannel underwear. He carried a clarinet.

After deliberation, adjustment, readjustment, and knocking

the thing over three times, they finally set up a music stand. The tall one produced a sheet of music from an enormous briefcase. With a fine flourish and a triumphant bow he placed it on the music stand. It promptly slid off. Just as the audience was becoming dangerously restive, the duet commenced.

They started out bravely enough, playing with tremendous verve until the tall one lost his place. The pink one carried on while his partner searched the music with a bony forefinger. When at last he got going the pink chap lost his place. This sort of thing went on for some time with the utmost solemnity. The audience was close to hysteria.

A farmer sitting next to us, whose shiny blue suit gave off a heady effluvium of cows, manure, and Sea Island mud, clutched his ribs and howled.

"Please," he managed to moan, "will somebody please ask them fellers to stop? They're killin' me!"

We should have known that our easygoing way of life was too good to last. We three had taken part in a school play the previous Christmas and our parents insisted that we repeat the performance at the local show. We attempted to dissuade them. The play, we pointed out, while based on the excellent poem "Père Lalemont," had not been greeted with thunderous applause. It had been, in point of fact, a dismal failure. Most of us had forgotten great chunks of our lines. Not that it made much difference because it was doubtful if our yeeping little voices had projected beyond the footlights.

Then there was the matter of costumes. No self-respecting Indians would have worn such outlandish outfits. Our relatives who made the costumes had relied entirely on their imaginations, choosing to ignore finicky research. The result was fifteen Huron braves each evidently belonging to fifteen different tribes that had never existed in the first place.

Makeup presented another problem. No amount of greasepaint could disguise our blue-eyed, Anglo Saxon, Irish and Scottish backgrounds.

All these arguments failed, of course. Arrangements were made for our appearance on stage. There followed ten evenings of frantic rehearsals and the washing and pressing of our weird getups.

With the relentless inevitability of fate in a Greek tragedy, Saturday night arrived. Sick with stage fright, we cowered in our dressing room while helpful parents dabbed on ineffectual makeup and bullied us about diction and the importance of final t's. We worried about only three of us carrying a play originally performed by the good Father Lalemont and supported by fifteen pseudo-Indians. Then somebody tapped on the door.

"Curtain call in five minutes."

We trooped out to wait in the wings. The curtain came down, and volunteer stagehands set up the scenery in a couple of minutes. In stage centre appeared a campfire of small logs with red tissue paper stuffed around them and a weak light bulb stuck in behind. There was a cardboard canoe painted to look something like birch bark against a backdrop of painted trees that looked like nothing in nature. We assumed our positions. The curtain rose. There was restrained applause.

Père Lalemont (Ernie), who had the only long speech, proceeded to harangue the savage Huron on the advantages of Christianity while we two stood "wolf-eyed, wolf-sinewed, more silent than the trees." We tried to look the part, but our wolf eyes were close to tears of frustration and our wolf sinews shivered uncontrollably.

Then it happened. With a grand gesture Ernie stepped backwards, knocked over the campfire, and fell sprawling onto the canoe. He flattened it properly. Our audience roared its appreciation. We leapt to Ernie's aid as an apparent short circuit transformed the fake campfire into a real one. Stagehands rushed out with buckets of water, soaking the fire and us with total lack of discrimination. In the wings frantic mothers wrung their hands.

Dripping wet and standing in puddles, we three recovered our aplomb. We stepped smartly to the footlights and bowed to the cheering crowd. We answered three curtain calls to thunderous applause. There is nothing so satisfying to an actor as audience appreciation. Better still, we knew that we should never again be asked to perform on stage.

*OUR
READING
HABITS*

*R*eading habits of the young have always caused some consternation among adults and invoked much learned discussion among academics. The truth is that children have always lived in a world of their own and have read anything that intrigued them. If adults would think back to their own childhood reading habits they would realize that there is no need for parental concern or academic debate. Let the kids read what they want to read. It is amazing how much they can learn.

Some young people never really acquire the reading habit. Others seem to concentrate on a specific subject. Gabby was one of those. As a youngster he devoured the sports page in the Vancouver *Sun* and drooled over the sporting goods section of Eaton's catalogue.

Ernie was an adventure story nut, particularly Canadian adventure. He could become totally absorbed in *Kazan; Baree, Son of Kazan* or any of the works of James Oliver Curwood. Torchy read non-fiction. When only twelve or thirteen he could read and fully understand scientific papers far beyond most adults' comprehension. He was forever baffling us with quiet monologues on the structure of vulcanite, or the muscular makeup of the common earthworm.

My own reading covered a wide variety of subjects—too wide perhaps, because I never became an expert on anything. We had a fine library at home which included contemporary novels and mysteries as well as the classics. My father was a learned man with an impressive list of fellowships and academic degrees. His library concentrated mainly on botany, but included a solid background in all of the biological sciences. He had everything there, from dull texts on craniology to a treatise on banana culture in Java. I can hear him now.

"Observe the parabolic shape of the supraorbital curve and

the rapid plunge to the basal region, an infallible way to identify a Labrador Eskimo skull."

My reading really began, I suppose, with *Black Beauty*, which was a good story. About this time I also read *Beautiful Joe*, a morbid yarn too reminiscent of a trite religious tract. Even at eight years old the thing made me quite ill. Seeking something more exciting I turned to *The Adventures of Billy Topsail,* an excellent yarn about a Newfoundland boy.

Most of our literature came from Britain. We had the *Boys' Own Annual* and *Chums.* Here were stories carefully researched and well written. We followed adventurous seamen and soldiers all over the Empire, fighting pirates on the Spanish Main, reliving the Sepoy Mutiny, or tracking mountain gorillas in the African rain forest.

There were good school stories, too, although some of the terminology was a bit puzzling. For instance, I never did learn what the fourth form was. It certainly was not the fourth grade. The boys were too old. No fourth-grader would be capable of dreaming up the unbelievable devilment of the lads in the fourth form at St. Dominic's.

Another favourite was the "penny dreadful." Penny dreadfuls were small books, badly written, poorly illustrated and only stapled together. They dwelled largely on detective stories which followed a standard pattern. Police Constable Watkins would discover a corpse in a dingy street—some poor bloke done in by person or persons unknown. Watkins was, of course, completely mystified. After filling two or three pages in his carefully written notebook, he would make his report to Chief Detective Inspector Applegate of Scotland Yard, an undoubted genius. Then followed a manhunt by scores of unhurried policemen in dripping raincapes while Big Ben boomed through the fog. The good Chief Inspector would find a single clue, perhaps a button wrenched from the victim's jacket or half a train ticket to Brighton. With nothing more to work on, Applegate would solve the mystery by applying pure intelligence in a way that made Sherlock Holmes appear feeble-minded.

Penny dreadful writers occasionally branched out into adventures about faraway places. I suspect that they were careful to locate the places as far away as possible in the hope that their readers had never travelled to them. Thus there was no need to worry about climatic conditions or topographical accuracy. Their stories of the Canadian wilderness, for example, were inaccurate beyond belief, and it is unlikely that the natives of the area would recognize their own country.

I had one story entitled *Blizzard Bill, the Dead Shot*. Blizzard Bill was depicted on the cover as a giant of a man with thigh-length leather boots, fringed buckskin jacket, and a hat large enough to shelter a flock of sheep. He leaned nonchalantly on a muzzle-loading musket about two yards long.

For page after page Blizzard Bill tracked the villain, Dark Dan, the Danite. Yes, those really were their names. The chase went on over burning desert and alkali flat. Dark Dan was no dummy. He lured Blizzard Bill into an all but impenetrable pine forest where Bill, master tracker though he was, was tested to the utmost. Of course, it all ended up in a shootout, at a range impossible even for a modern sniper with the world's most sophisticated weapon.

In our house we had complete sets of Mark Twain and Dickens, two writers who could be read over and over and always seem fresh and entertaining. *Tom Sawyer* has been called the immortal story of a boy, and so it is. *Oliver Twist* had the power to change the inhuman child labour laws in Britain.

Those old-time writers told their tales vividly, and their characters were living, breathing people. They wrote about a country they knew, an era they thoroughly understood. Their stories will never die.

The mystery writers of my time were craftsmen. Some of them, it is true, used the character combination that was so successful in the Sherlock Holmes stories: that of the brilliant detective and his not-too-bright assistant. Nevertheless, their plots were very good indeed. Agatha Christie had her Hercule Poirot and Captain Hastings, and she never wrote a bad book. Earl Derr Bigger's Charlie Chan was pure entertainment. We had Asy Mayo, the Cape Cod Sherlock. Sax Rohmer's *Brood of the Witch Queen* actually had me looking over my shoulder.

During my youth, mystery writers created their detectives with humour and human feelings, and made them intelligent but not super-intelligent. Unlike the "heroes" of modern detective fiction, they were never brutal for the sake of brutality. Today, the story line tends towards tortured nudes in blood-spattered rooms, with the private eye solving his case by killing everybody in the hope that one of his bullet-riddled corpses is the bad guy.

We had no comic books as such. There were comic strips in the daily newspapers, of course, and a large cartoon section on weekends. For the most part, the strips were anything but comical. Little Orphan Annie and the characters surrounding her were never guilty of the faintest glimmer of humour. *Bringing Up Father,* featuring Maggie and Jiggs, was not much better. We were bludgeoned by the heavy humour of the Katzenjammer Kids. If we wanted real humour we turned to the noted wits of the time. Who could forget P.G. Wodehouse, with his Bertie Wooster and Jeeves? Mr. Colin Glencannon was Guy Gilpatric's whisky-drinking hero and chief engineer of the

S.S. *Inchcliffe Castle.* There has been nothing before or since Gilpatric's time to equal the Glencannon stories.

Our homes would have been inundated with magazines had we succumbed to salesmen's blandishments. We had to be selective. Torchy started out with *Popular Science* and *Popular Mechanics.* He soon graduated to material of such scientific complexity that we had difficulty reading the titles, much less the contents. Torchy would spend hours on pages of mathematics, and then attempt to explain them to us. He found me particularly obtuse. I have always fought a losing battle with simple arithmetic and never once made a passing grade in algebra.

Gabby spent heavily on sports magazines. He had an encyclopaedic memory for all sorts of useless information, or so it seemed to me. He always knew who won what hockey game and why. He could quote the batting averages of every major league ballplayer in North America. He knew all about soccer, skating, and field lacrosse. At least Gabby was an authority on something, a feat which I secretly envied.

Ernie's literary tastes were much like mine. He bought *Field and Stream.* I had *Outdoor Life,* and we swapped. We both cut out hundreds of coupons and sent away for anything that was free. I still have a waterproof, floatable match case advertising Duxbac hunting togs that I sent for in 1930. We had a complete collection of gun catalogues: Winchester, Remington, Savage, Colt, and the rest. I sent for a catalogue dealing with the Thompson submachine gun—and got it, much to my surprise. The full page ad in the magazine was a little frightening. It showed a cowboy dashing out of a cabin and giving the rustlers their come uppance with a Thompson Model 25A. He was emptying saddles right, left, and centre in a blaze of gunfire and a shower of ejected cartridge cases. The weapon was advertised as having the accuracy of a rifle and the portability of a pistol and was recommended, believe it or not, for hunting.

We did not bother with fishing tackle catalogues. Living close to the sea we knew something about cod, salmon, and the rest. We caught trout on the Fraser sandbars. The catalogues we could have sent for dealt in tackle suitable for eastern U.S. conditions. There were fancy lures for bluegills, perch, sunfish, black bass. The illustrations of those fish failed to excite us. They seemed such piddling little things compared with a spring salmon.

Ernie and I did not read outdoor magazines exclusively. *Saturday Evening Post, Argosy, Blackwood's Magazine* and *National Geographic* all offered good, solid reading material. There was some good radio entertainment on rainy winter evenings, and since television had not been invented, we read a great deal to pass the time. Maybe we even learned a thing or two. Could be.

MY
ATHLETIC
CAREER

*A*s a youngster I could run like a cheetah, and I have always been deadly with any kind of firearm. But I am a hopeless duffer at games. Any games at all. Soccer, cards, dominoes, baseball, eightball, checkers, tiddlywinks. My one attempt at golf proved that I could dig holes in the ground faster and deeper than the Vancouver City Sewer Department.

Gabby played good softball and first-class soccer, but ice hockey was really his game. Ernie was a gymnast. Torchy was a scholar who had no interest in games. I was neither scholar nor gamester, but I tried. Man, how I tried. In the eighth grade somebody organized a soccer team. We applicants were taken onto the field to see what we could do. Gabby was selected immediately to play outside right. I tripped over my feet. With a sigh of despair the coach pointed to the goal.

"See what you can do in there, Ashlee. With your height you might be of some value."

I was not. Playing against a rival school one Saturday I made such a fool of myself that I was fired on the spot. That day, either our team was extremely good or our opposition was extremely bad. All the action stayed at the opposite end of the field. Having nothing to do I was leaning against a goal post chatting to Joany MacGregor when a wild yell went up from the crowd. Recovering with an effort from Joany's piquant charm, I spun around to see the ball rolling slowly through the exact centre of the goal. The coach pointed a finger and jerked a thumb. I retired to boos from the gallery and sighs of relief from my teammates.

A few weeks later a local businessman offered to sponsor a softball team. In what he hoped was good public relations and a real effort to keep us from hanging around street corners, he called us together.

"I'm an old-time ballplayer," he announced. "Played for several championship teams."

"I'll bet," I thought. "Champions of Gopher Gulch, Alberta, population forty-one."

"I'm going to whip you into shape. Now show me how you can run."

We lined up. Our new coach yelled and we took off at top speed. There was nothing to it. The "cheetah" loped in yards ahead of the pack. The coach nodded with satisfaction and selected two teams.

Our lot was first up to bat. The rival pitcher took a threatening stance on the mound. He was a redheaded boy, left-handed and very strong for his age. He wound up and let fly. The ball whistled over the plate at what looked like about five hundred feet per second. The batter never saw it and the catcher was driven back three paces. Our coach whooped with glee. He had really found himself a ballplayer.

The second pitch was as fast or faster. Unfortunately, the ball whizzed over the backstop, disappeared into a hardhack swamp and was never seen again. A new ball was tossed to the pitcher. He paused before going into his flamboyant windup. His bristly red eyebrows met over a scowl of pure menace. The batter poised nervously. The pitch. The ball struck the ground halfway to home plate and ricocheted erratically with a great chunk of cover flapping in the breeze. The coach contained his impatience.

"No good, kid," he said. "You have all kinds of speed but no control. We'll work on it."

He selected a new pitcher. Gabby stepped up to the plate and at the first pitch casually belted out a double. The next kid got two strikes before making a single. My turn. Carefully selecting the thickest bat on the theory that it would have the

53

best chance of connecting with the ball, I imitated Gabby's stance and eyed the field. The boy on first was poised for action. Gabby knew better. He was not getting ready to run anywhere. The pitch. Straight over the plate at exactly the right height. I stepped into it. Crack! The bat connected as no other bat has done before or since. The ball soared over the heads of the farthest outfielders. I trotted home to loud cheers from the gallery. The loudest of all came from our coach.

"You'll be our star slugger," he yelled.

Gabby and Ernie exchanged knowing looks.

At succeeding games my efforts excited much comment, but all of it was on the debit side. The simple truth is that I was struck out regularly. If I managed to hit the ball it was foul or a pop fly that dropped square into a fielder's glove. Our coach wrung his hands and rolled his eyes heavenwards.

"I hate to say this, kid," he groaned, " but you'll never make it as a ballplayer. Ever thought of making model airplanes?"

I had the good sense to resign. Model airplanes were out, though. Even if I were interested, there was no point in trying to compete with a champion. His name was Ross Farquarson.

Gabby claimed that Ross only had to write his initials on a piece of wood and it would fly. He was not far wrong. Whether his models were driven by tiny gasoline engines or wound-up rubber bands made no difference. His non- flying models were a joy to look at. A meticulous craftsman who worked to precise scale, he entered every possible competition and won at a canter. I remember when Fisher Bodies sponsored a contest, open to youngsters in Canada and the United States, to build a model of Napoleon's coach. Ross won over all entrants. He was whisked away to Detroit to learn car body design. We never saw or heard of him again, but there was no doubt in our minds that he was a complete success.

I never attempted ice hockey. I did not own skates, and with so many vivid memories of past athletic failures, I hesitated to buy a pair. Gabby was good at it. The firemen at Number 22 Hall in Marpole sponsored his team. The coach and general factotum was Moose Robinson, a great guy. Why he was called "Moose" I will never understand. He was short and stout. I towered over him. By sheer force of personality, and a genuine rapport with young people, Moose coached a seldom defeated team. I went to the games wearing a team sweater.

Moose Robinson knew all about hockey and nothing about boats. He and a couple of friends acquired a fourteen foot, flat-bottomed derelict and worked for days making it seaworthy. One Saturday morning they filled the seams with tar, turned the boat right side up, and left a garden hose running in it to swell the seams. Then they went downtown to celebrate their success. Eight hours and five pubs later the Moose remembered the boat and the water running into it. Fearing that the weight of water would split the hull the three celebrants rushed home, expecting the worst. They found the hose still running, the boat bone dry, and the lawn under it a quagmire.

"I guess," said Moose, "that tar ain't no good without something to pour it onto. We should have used some of that stuff, what d'y'call it? Caulking cotton?"

Many years later Moose was killed in a fire department accident. Youngsters in whom he had taken an interest dropped everything to attend his funeral, which was the largest Vancouver had ever seen. Moose would have liked that.

I attempted other games, such as five pin bowling. However, it was obvious from the start that bowling was not my game. It was much too noisy, for one thing. To an ear attuned to listening to a blue grouse scratching among dead leaves ten yards away, the crash and clatter of the alley was torture. Nor could I see any point in standing up a lot of bits of wood just to knock them down again. Exit bowling.

In a brilliant flash of mental illumination I finally recognized a fact which had been obvious to others for years. I would never learn to play games even moderately well. Better to develop real aptitudes. Some of my paintings had been displayed at the PNE. Kid stuff, admittedly, but one has to start somewhere. While Gabby and Ernie sat by the radio intent on a Canadiens-Maple Leafs game, I spent many happy hours overhauling a model '94 Winchester and listening to Beethoven's Ninth. To each his own.

THE
JOKER

*I*t grieves me to report that we of the ninth grade were typical of our age group in our approach to education. Like that of Grade Niners in every generation, our behaviour in class was something less than exemplary. We played jokes on our teachers and classmates. We were punished, but punishment failed to curb the workings of our devious minds. In truth, most of our pranks were harmless enough. No victim of our practical pleasantries was ever injured or suffered permanent embarrassment. The worst that can be said is that we were a disruptive force. What teacher could explain the propositions of Euclid to a class doubled up with laughter because Ernie had released a mechanical tarantula on Joany MacGregor's desk?

Then there was the painful affair resulting from Gabby's experiment in physics class. For some unaccountable reason Gabby had unscrewed the caps from a case of bronze weights. He discovered that each weight was partially filled with small pellets of lead, like bird shot. With satanic purpose he poured a portion of shot out of one weight into another. And another. Then he started over again. The result was, of course, that when our teacher demonstrated an experiment involving precise weight, the project was a dismal failure. We watched gleefully as Mr. Watson struggled without success to adjust his scales. Typically, Gabby confessed to the crime and spent many after- school hours with scales and a set of master weights, re-evaluating the set he had disrupted.

There was one teacher we did not fool around with. He was a lean and hungry looking six-footer with eyes like death rays. He always had absolute control of his class. His weapon was sarcasm, and even Alec Carmichael, the most obnoxious joker of all, cringed before Mr. O'Neil's searching gaze and vitriolic tongue.

"If you were clothed to suit your mentality, Carmichael, you would be wearing diapers and not the flamboyant finery you have seen fit to exhibit today."

The point was well taken. Carmichael's dress was always the extreme in fashion. History, particularly in the matter of dress, repeats itself. In the late twenties and early thirties it was fashionable for the younger set to wear trousers something like today's flairs, only more so. Twenty-six-inch bell bottoms were not uncommon. Yet they were not wide enough to suit Carmichael. By having a couple of gussets sewn into each trouser leg he extended the cuff measurement to thirty-two inches. He was small for his age, and his feet disappeared completely under yards of flapping cloth.

Wide ties were the rage. Carmichael sported a handmade creation which all but covered his narrow chest. Unable to find a tie pin worthy of such a tie, he had Torchy solder a pin onto a bicycle reflector. Never one to do things by halves, our Torchy added a flashlight bulb with wires running to a switch and a couple of batteries concealed in Carmichael's pocket. It was the brilliant flash of red light from the tie pin which had inspired Mr. O'Neil's caustic comment.

Alec Carmichael was a type that parents refer to as a nasty little boy. He took pride in being nicknamed "The Joker." Many of his pranks were amusing but there were occasions when he went too far. Such as the time he stuck his foot through the ceiling.

Our school had first been built as a two-room affair in 1911. By the time Gabby, Ernie, and I enrolled in that institute of higher learning, a fine brick building to house eight hundred students had been constructed. The original school, known as the woodshed, had not been torn down. This was just as well, because as the student body increased in size, and the school did not, basement space was made over into classrooms, and then the "woodshed" on the far side of the school yard was reopened.

We were there one Monday morning with heads bowed low, not in reverence, but to get closer to a completely incomprehensible problem in algebra.

Thump, thump, thump.

We straightened up, alarmed by a noise directly overhead. Shivering howls of ghostly laughter accompanied the repeated thumping. Thump, thump, thump. Crash! A shoe which we all recognized for its small size and modish design came through the ceiling. Carmichael attempted to withdraw his foot, the splintered laths sprang upward, and The Joker, hopelessly trapped, began yelling piteously for help.

The teacher summoned the school janitor. Working from the top of a high stepladder he hacked away with a claw hammer until Carmichael was free. He was taken first to the medical room to be treated for numerous cuts and abrasions. The offender's next stop was the principal's office, where he was threatened with expulsion unless his behaviour improved. He was also ordered to pay repair costs.

This incident should have cured Carmichael of his practical joking. But it did not. Feeling no remorse for the havoc he had created or for the damage that his parents had been compelled to pay for, The Joker continued his depredations. One winter's day he sat shivering in class. When the teacher asked what was the matter, he complained that the room was cold. Sure enough, the thermometer registered only forty-eight degrees. The teacher telephoned the engineer, who stoked up the old coal-burning furnace until the school felt like a sauna bath. We found out later that Carmichael had wedged a piece of ice behind the thermometer.

And so it went. In one classroom where a teacher solemnly

intoned the conjugations of Latin verbs, a loud explosion interrupted his discourse and the fragments of a plaster bust of Voltaire filled the air. The cause was discovered to be a large firecracker with a long fuse. It was a typical Carmichael gesture, but who could prove it? He was with us in room thirty-one on the floor above.

When he flattened both tires on Torchy's bike, The Joker went too far. If he had tried something like that with the inseparable three our vengeance would have been dire, and Carmichael knew it. He also knew that he was safe from the non-militant and inoffensive Torchy. He should have realized that our Torchy was not alone. He had friends in great numbers, including his brother Gabby, Ernie, and me.

Torchy's discovery of the culprit was a shrewd bit of detective work. He examined the several inner tube punctures and found the sharp end of a bronze pin which he thought he recognized. When Carmichael was in gym strip, Torchy got hold of the bike-reflector tie pin he had made for The Joker. The point was broken off and the fragment fitted. Clear evidence, indeed. Torchy brought the problem to us. We held a council of war.

It was decided that we three would go after Carmichael unmercifully. We would devise one practical joke after another until The Joker became a nervous wreck and begged us to desist. At lunchtime the very next day Carmichael discovered that the sandwiches he had looked forward to so hungrily had undergone a drastic change. Ernie had managed to replace the sliced ham with neat squares of red rubber. At the same time he had transformed the mustard into yellow showcard paint. Carmichael fumed impotently, knowing full well who was responsible. He dared not attack us physically. Gabby could put him down with one hand, and on three occasions I had picked him up and shaken him until his teeth rattled.

The following morning Carmichael charged into industrial arts class, late as usual, and grabbed his nail apron on the dead run. There was a ripping sound and The Joker found himself staring at an apron torn into five pieces. Gabby had nailed it to the bench. At that instant Ernie strolled up behind Carmichael and shoved a bottle of water, open end down, into his hip pocket.

Carmichael finally realized that he had walked into a situation which he could not handle. That must have been a severe shock to his ego. He avoided us as much as he could, which was not really surprising. We kept after him. As the Easter vacation approached, Carmichael became more and more subdued. He who had demanded and expected unremitting attention flitted quietly around the school, unobtrusive as the meekest of mice. We had won, or so we believed.

For a few days our thoughts were occupied with Easter exams and the approaching ten-day vacation. It must be admitted that the latter was uppermost in our minds, although we did do some studying. I struggled with mathematical problems that Torchy could do in his head. Torchy wore a frown of intense concentration trying to memorize classical poems that I could reel off by the yard. Gabby and Ernie were good, steady, B-average students. The Joker behaved himself.

When all the examination papers had been turned in, we relaxed in the glowing anticipation of a ten-day reprieve. We, the inseparable three, made plans. As always the Fraser River drew us like a magnet. The unseasonably warm weather promised early swimming. We knew where huge sturgeon lurked on the muddy river bottom, and there was a good chance of catching Dolly Varden trout on the sandbars close to shore. Always the craftsman, our Torchy was anxious to complete his superbly hand-crafted rowboat. Gabby's mention of baseball was received with a notable lack of enthusiasm. Ernie boasted of having all his fishing tackle ready and waiting—lines cleaned and coiled, lead sinkers newly cast, and hooks honed needle sharp. My new .22 rifle needed to be sighted in. In this joyous mood we felt so kindly toward the whole world that we ceased to heckle The Joker.

When the final bell rang, nearly a thousand students rushed cheerfully out of the school. They carried such items as lunch kits, sports equipment, and winter clothing dredged from the dark recesses of their lockers. There was not one textbook to be seen. Carmichael led the mob, running as fast as his super-bell bottoms would permit.

Torchy leapt onto his bike, pushed down hard on a pedal and the chain parted. The bike and Torchy landed in a tangled heap of spinning wheels and flailing limbs. We rushed to his rescue. He was shaken but unhurt. A quick examination of the broken chain showed that the master link had been removed and replaced with soft copper wire painted black. Torchy's bike was fitted with a large leather combination tool bag and oddments container hanging from the saddle. Gabby reached into it for the spare master link he knew would be there, let out a scream of rage and pain, jerked his hand out of the bag and danced about howling, with three fingers gripped in a gopher trap. The Joker had had the last laugh.

PARDONNEZ
US

*I*mbéciles!" M.Carpentier screamed hysterically "Des têtes de bois, vous!"

We were in the ninth grade at the time, struggling with the intricacies of the French language. We had learned a few words but were unable to string them together in a way that made sense. We were completely baffled by verbs, both regular and irregular. The short sentences that we had memorized—"This is the pen of my aunt," or "The teacher stands at the back of the class"— did not make for scintillating conversation. In fact, we were making no headway whatever. Our high-strung instructor had reached the limit of his patience with our individual and collective stupidity.

"Monsieur Gabby," moaned M. Carpentier, "you not only have the thickest head in this class but you appear to be tongue-tied. Now repeat after me. Est-ce que le soleil brille? Non, il ne brille pas de soleil. And don't forget the 'de.' Répétez, s'il vous plaît. Plus vite!"

Gabby, so named because he seldom said anything, even in English, was literally struck dumb when confronted by another language. He just sat there while M. Carpentier heaped abuse upon him, maintaining throughout the wordless stolidity of a stuffed owl.

"Class, I have an idea," said the teacher. "Not brilliant, not even original, but a scheme that has worked before. I want you to talk to each other in French as best you can. Tell each other off. Indulge in name calling. Anything. But no English, please."

As M. Carpentier reached into his desk drawer for his aspirins, Ernie turned to Joan MacGregor.

"Joany, ma chérie," he murmured romantically, "je t'adore, je t'adore."

"Shut it yourself, Ernie," snapped Joany. "Y'crippled?"

Pandemonium. When M. Carpentier had restored some

semblance of order, he addressed us sadly.

"Class," he croaked, "it could be that you are neither more nor less stupid and unreceptive than the average of your age and experience. If that is so, then I am not getting through to you and I have failed as a school teacher. Perhaps I should be more successful teaching at the university level. In any case there is no point in my trying to carry on here. I go now to the principal's office to tender my resignation. Au revoir, mes amis."

He left, closing the door softly behind him. We sat in shocked silence, for we liked Armand Carpentier in spite of our treatment of him.

In the spirited discussion following our teacher's departure we tried to decide whether he was kidding us, or whether we had destroyed a real human being. Impassioned debate failed to settle the question, although most of us felt that M. Carpentier had meant what he said. He usually did. We resolved to send him a letter apologizing for our behaviour and asking him to reconsider his resignation. Moreover, we would write the letter in French. As best we could, anyway.

There was much frantic searching through textbooks and English-French, French-English dictionaries. The letter, we felt, had to be brief. It had to be sincere, totally devoid of maudlin sentimentality, and in terminology worthy of the most experienced diplomat.

"First we must apologize for all the horsing around," said Gabby. "What's French for horsing around?"

"Chevaling around?" Ernie suggested.

"Be dignified, you apes," said Joany MacGregor, riffling through a dictionary. "We should say something classy like 'we offer you the olive branch.' What's the French expression?"

"Au pied de la lettre," says I, looking smug.

After several false starts, rewrites, and spelling corrections, our letter was ready for delivery. Our classmates were unanimous in their decision to send Gabby, Ernie, and me because, they proclaimed with unflattering honesty, we were the worst of a bad lot and an apology from us would really mean something. Joany MacGregor was selected to represent the girls and lend a little glamour to the group.

When we entered the principal's office it was immediately apparent to us that M. Carpentier had actually resigned his position. We could tell by the way the principal's eyes played over us, scorching our hair.

Joany smiled prettily and curtseyed gracefully, although we three considered that gesture a bit overdone, and presented M. Carpentier with our letter. He studied it with the alert caution of a mongoose confronted by a cobra.

"Cher M. Carpentier," he read aloud. "We, la classe dans room 31 hereby apologize pour notre imbécile behaviour and chevaling around. Nous désirons que vous recall votre resignation. Nous offer au pied de la lettre. S'il vous plaît, monsieur, returnez a la classe et pardonnez us."

Everyone in the class had signed the letter.

"Eh, bien," said M. Carpentier, tearing his letter of resignation into small fragments, "I shall return to la classe number thirty-one and attempt to teach you something. You must make one solemn promise: no more chevaling around."

He whooped with laughter. So did the principal. It was good to hear them.

MARSHLAND
SAGA

W e must have looked ridiculous, Swede and I, tramping through the reeds with shotguns and full equipment, preceded by three waddling mallards. That was in the day when live decoys were legal and Andy, Min and Silent Susie, brave with neat leather collars and codline leashes, were supposed to swim in a tidal pool, looking so alluring that they would entice vast flocks within range of our weaponry.

Our day had started early, horribly early. It was 4 a.m. when I arrived at Swede's home to find him cooking breakfast, so I joined him in his meal of bacon and eggs, the second for me within the hour. After the dishes were stacked and ready for Swede's sisters to wash, we collected our gear and the three tame mallards and walked briskly to the river two miles away. From there it was simply a matter of rowing five miles to Iona Island near the mouth of the Fraser.

All week long the weather had been the sort that duck hunters dream about. Rain drummed down incessantly and the southeast wind sang in the marshes, driving the ducks and snow geese to the sheltered ponds hidden in the bullrush swamps. Naturally, as Swede and I struggled against the flooding tide, the sun broke through the cloud cover, the wind dropped to a whisper and the ducks, every mother's son of them, headed out to sea. We kept going, regardless, being among those for whom hope springs eternal.

A word about the boat. She was a twelve-foot, hard chine, displacement hull built by Gabby's brother Torchy. Even as a teenager Torchy was a craftsman and a perfectionist whose woodwork was a joy to behold. Products of his basement shop clearly portrayed the soul of an artist and a mathematician. His furniture had a finish worthy of the finest English gun stocks and an accuracy usually reserved for pattern makers.

He had scrounged boat building material from the river. He

found a long, straight-grained slab of red cedar which he hand split and planed to precisely one-half inch. His frames were made of yellow cedar; knees and breast hook from wind-twisted Garry oak. I can see him now, ankle deep in fragrant cedar shavings, as he fashioned his oars with a razor-sharp draw knife. A craftsman and a perfectionist and something of a loner, that was our Torchy.

Swede and I anchored his tame ducks in a sheltered pond and concealed ourselves some thirty yards away, hoping for the best. We sat for an hour; the October sun burned hot, and soon we shucked off hunting jackets and flannel shirts. The inaction became a bit wearisome, when we could see mallards by the hundreds a mile out at sea.

Leaving Andy, Min, and Silent Susie to their own devices, we wandered away, hoping to scare up a non-seagoing duck or two which had remained behind to feed in the swamp. We discovered none, but when a flock of snipe swirled out of the reeds seventy yards away I let drive with my old twelve-bore just out of spite. They were hopelessly out of range, but much to my surprise I got one of them.

Having collected the snipe, we turned back towards our duck pond. As we broke through the bullrushes at the edge of the clearing, we could see the three anchored mallards dozing peacefully and not far off, two hunters sneaking up on them.

We began to yell and scream. The hunters heeded not, intent upon the business at hand. We ran for the pond. I fired a warning shot which caught the interlopers' attention and gave them pause. That was enough to avert tragedy, but Swede's Viking blood was up. With a war cry straight from one of the more murderous Norse sagas, he went for the enemy. Waving his shotgun, his blonde locks bouncing wildly, he charged through the knee deep pool, scattering the ducks. I followed, screaming hoarsely. (I, too, have some Viking ancestry, and was not to be outdone.) To be attacked by one wild man was startling enough for the hunters; two was more than they could tolerate. They turned and ran and, in spite of their heavy clothing and hip waders, made such a turn of speed we could never have caught them. When they were out of sight and sound, Swede and I collapsed beside the pond and laughed until our ribs ached.

We hitched a ride home by tying the boat to the end of a log boom being towed up river. It was a slow way of getting there, but much less arduous than rowing.

With nothing to show for our day's outing but one miserable little snipe we trudged to Swede's place, carrying the three tame ducks, and decided that we would never again use live decoys. It was too nerve-wracking. Wooden decoys would have to serve. Perhaps Torchy would carve the heads for us, expertly, artistically, with that special touch of genius that would make them seem alive. Of course he would. We had only to ask.

THE
CAMP
COOK

W had pitched camp beside a sparkling mountain stream somewhere southeast of Cultus Lake, and Ernie, who considered himself a real hotshot of a camp cook, served breakfast. He handed out plates of leathery, grease-encrusted eggs, slabs of bread thick with lumps of butter, and tin cups of tea strong enough to tan moose hide. With an appetite for anything, of which only the young and the starving are capable, we wolfed down this culinary triumph—but diluted it later with generous draughts of water from the stream.

How we managed to find ourselves in that gentle wilderness sixty miles from home calls for some explanation. We had reached the age of mobility. I had acquired a 1924 Model T two-door sedan, after much haggling, for eighteen dollars and a Webley revolver. That old car was an impressive piece of machinery. She stood six feet five in her smooth tires, with a Ruckstell axle, Rocky Mountain brakes—and a right rear wheel which had a tendency to fall off. Motoring in those days was an adventure quite unlike the numbing experience endured on today's freeways in an automatic, power-steered, powerbraked, thin-shelled monster, where the driver's only scenery is the brake light on the car ahead.

Fixing the back wheel so that it stayed put called for considerable ingenuity. Being neither mechanic nor blacksmith, and ignoring finicky science, I went straight to the heart of the problem, as novices often do. I hacksawed the axle nut in two and tightened it in place, applying as much strain as the almost stripped threads on the axle would stand. Then I set up a blowtorch. The roaring blue flame blistered the remaining paint on the wooden wheel spokes, but the axle soon glowed cherry red. A few heavy blows with a ball peen hammer made a riveting job as secure as a ship's plate. I have sometimes wondered how the next owner managed to remove the wheel.

So now we sat around the campfire, sipping Ernie's corrosive tea and discussing cookery. Since we were part of an era which existed long before instant coffee, biscuit mixes, and the like, we were compelled, despite having no aptitude for it, to cope with raw materials as best we could. We occasionally ate raw dandelion leaves or stewed stinging nettle. We boiled grouse. The flavour varied from bad to worse, depending on what our Siwash lapool (Chinook jargon for grouse) had been feeding on. If the bird had known a diet of blueberries, it was not so bad, but if it had been on a fir-bud feeding spree, the boiled fowl smelled and tasted exactly like pitch.

A ten-pound bag of flour was a staple, as were canned beans, plenty of bacon and butter—marble-hard or flowing greasily, depending on the weather. We obtained a basic flour and water mixture by pushing a fist into the flour, filling the hollow with creek water, and mixing with the fingers. To this we added a pinch of baking soda, if we happened to have some with us, and a little salt. What this mixture finally became depended on the solidity of the mix—if fairly gooey, it was baked into bannock bread; if runny, flapjacks.

Ernie held forth at some length about the futility and time-consuming labour involved in baking one thin bannock at a time. He assured us that he could produce an edible loaf of such proportions as to keep us fed for a five-day trip. That evening, after a good day tramping the sun-dappled woods, hunting and fishing with modest success, Gabby and I prepared a fire pit while Ernie mixed his bannock.

Using all the remaining flour, about seven pounds, and adding salt (but no baking soda because we had forgotten to bring any), he soon built a good, solid dough, which he stuffed into a large aluminum pot.

When the fire had died down to red coals, we buried the pot

to the rim, covered the coals with a thick layer of earth to keep the heat in, and retired to our beds of blankets and fir boughs. We hoped that the fire would last all night, and that by the morning the bannock would be well done and golden crusted, as Ernie confidently predicted it would be.

The fire held all night, which was more than we had expected. Ernie gingerly lifted his bannock from the hot ashes and shook it from the pot. Except for numerous bits of cinder adhering to it, the crust was golden brown. Gabby unsheathed his hunting knife to cut off a slice. Nothing happened. He bore down with all his strength. The knife skidded across the crust, leaving a faint scratch. I swung a hatchet, which rebounded as from a seasoned block of maple. Ernie said nothing.

As if on cue, Gabby stood the loaf on a stump and we shot at it. The .22 bullets penetrated an inch or so. Gabby's .30-30 fared better. My Lee-Enfield, using a 215 grain soft nose bullet, tore an ugly hole right through, but otherwise the bannock remained intact.

It may be there yet, that bannock, weathered and toughened by sun and storm, an object to bend the beaks of crows, blunt a pack rat's teeth, and defy the black bear's tearing claws. I must go back there, some day, and take a look.

CARLO

*F*irst we must launch the dog," said Torchy, approaching the problem scientifically. "One infallible method is to lure him onto a greasy plank with a steak."

Since we lacked both greasy plank and steak, we tried coaxing, wheedling, and, finally, yelling. Carlo, the golden cocker pup, flatly refused to launch himself into the muddy Fraser River. Attempting to ignore the gibes of my companions, I tucked Carlo under my arm and headed through the bush to Garfey's Pond. Gabby, Ernie, and Torchy trailed along, hurling insults. Had I acquired a lap dog, a mere pet, a canine sissy? With the duck-hunting season only eight months away the situation was desperate. Get busy, Ashlee, train the animal.

I hadn't the vaguest idea how to train a dog. Garfey's Pond seemed as good a place as any to make the attempt. Mirror calm, warmer than the river, nestled in an alder and vine maple wilderness, the pond had a soothing effect on the pup. I held him an inch or so above the water. He stopped shivering and began to make swimming motions. I lowered him gently into the water. He swam a short distance, scrambled ashore, shook himself, and returned to the pond. Within an hour Carlo was swimming with such enthusiasm that it took all our persuasiveness to get him out.

Carlo learned his trade rapidly and well. As his size and strength increased, he could crash through bullrushes as easily as through tall grass. He would retrieve a feathered dummy bird thrown into the thickest brushwood jungle.

He would retrieve anything. One Sunday we were fishing a Fraser sandbar in company with several men whom we did not know. We used short lines, dropping our worm-loaded hooks on a bar not thirty feet from shore. We picked up an occasional Dolly Varden, much to the outspoken chagrin of our fellow fishermen. They knew nothing about the river. Flinging their heavily weighted hand lines far beyond the sand, they caught nothing but mudsuckers. In impotent rage one chap wrenched a sucker from the hook and threw it back with all his strength. Carlo promptly dove in and retrieved it.

It was the first time that the cocker had retrieved a fish. He refused to give it up. He headed homewards and we followed, having no choice in the matter. We had to pass the interurban station at 64th Avenue, and found it crowded with women and children dressed in their Sunday best. With his head held high and exuding pride of accomplishment, Carlo trotted through the crowd, wiping fish slime onto silk stockings and little girls' dresses. We four prudently circled screaming women and sobbing tots, and tried to pretend that we did not know the dog, an act that fooled no one. Carlo carried on and, affecting not to notice swinging handbags and lunging parasols, went his dignified way.

At home, we persuaded Carlo to give up his fish. Ernie dropped it into a bucket of cold water, where it revived in minutes. We were ecstatic with this testimony to Carlo's gentle handling. We knew we had found a dog that could carry a duck without disturbing a feather.

Carlo's training, as we liked to think of it, continued all summer. Actually, no training was necesssary. The dog just did in his own way what he was born to do. He had a will of his own. He did not respond to punishment as most dogs do. We never beat him, of course, and he answered occasional slaps with a defiant snarl. Quite accidentally, however, I discovered a punishment that brought instant obedience. All I had to do was take his collar away. I had bought that brass-studded collar after saving spare cash for several weeks. Carlo wore it with pride. I took it from him for some reason I have now forgotten, and his shame was indescribable. He hung his head and looked utterly miserable. After that, I had no trouble getting him to do exactly as I wished. I scrounged some light harness leather from a tack shop and made a shoulder harness for him. It was quite a work of art, with a polished brass buckle and copper rivets. Carlo was as delighted as a youngster with a new cowboy outfit. He actually strutted around the neighbourhood showing off his new neckware.

It was then, as it is now, illegal to hunt ducks with a rifle. We realized that the law was based on sound common sense. We could readily imagine a crowd of hunters with deer rifles shooting over flat land and water. The ricochets alone would rapidly and drastically reduce the hunter population. On the million-to-one chance that a flying duck would be hit, there would be nothing left but skin and feathers.

Ernie owned a nice sixteen-gauge Ithaca double. Gabby was adequately armed and Torchy had no interest in firearms or hunting. That left me weaponless and financially flat as usual. While I was walking down Granville Street one morning, a garage mechanic friend hailed me and handed me a set of barrels, a stock, a forearm, and a jam tin full of parts for a Fox Sterlingworth twelve-gauge.

"Here," he said. "If you can put this thing together you can have it." My first thought was that he must not be much of a mechanic, but I realized in an instant that this was his way of making me a gift without embarrassing either of us. That turned out to be a good gun, far-reaching and easy to shoot.

Carlo's first season as a duck retriever was sensational. He never lost a bird, not even a cripple. January turned cold. Carlo would swim powerfully through drifting ice to collect a bird. Under ordinary circumstances we would never have permitted him to swim in such cold water. Fortunately, we knew every fisherman and woodcutter living in float houses along the river bank. We would visit one of them, present our host with a brace of duck, and be invited in for coffee. Carlo always headed straight for the stove. It must have been the right thing to do, for even when he grew old, deaf, and nearly blind there was no sign of stiffness or rheumatism.

Later that winter Carlo encountered solid ice for the first time. The adventure almost ended a beautiful friendship. Garfey's Pond had frozen over. Gabby wanted to check it out and try to estimate how many skaters it would support. As we sized up the situation Carlo trotted up with a stick to be thrown. Without thinking, I threw it, and it skittered across the ice. Carlo took a long dive and landed a real belly whopper. Eyes bulging and legs spread-eagled, he whirled in dizzy circles across the slick surface. He struggled to his feet, fell heavily, and lurched upright awkwardly. He tried running and pirouetted like Sonja Heinie at her Olympic best. When he stopped spinning he just stood a moment or two and thought it out. With infinite caution Carlo took a tentative step or two. Mincing across the ice like a careful drunk on a waxed dance floor, he eventually made shore, gave me one withering look, and trotted home on his own. He refused to speak to me for three days.

That winter was one of the coldest on record. Usually our winters meant continuous rain when every patch of ground became a bog and the Fraser River islands were flooded. In February the Fraser froze over. The sternwheeler *Sampson* gave up all attempts at ice-breaking. The *Sampson* was a flat-bottomed vessel with a unique approach to keeping the channel clear. She would charge headlong at a floe, slide well up onto it, and wait there until her weight smashed the ice.

Everyone who owned a pair of skates rushed down to the

river. Joyous prairie people demonstrated figure skating, and we watched them enviously. Impromptu hockey games started up all over the place. Some caution was necessary. The ice was several inches thick, but here and there were holes anywhere from two to forty feet across. The larger ones were easily identified: they were solidly packed with bluebill ducks.

One of our gang studied the ducks. He was a little guy under five feet tall and the same age as the rest of us, sixteen or seventeen. He decided to do some duck hunting. We tried hard to dissuade him. Too dangerous, we argued, with all those skaters whizzing around. Ignoring our pleas for sensible behaviour, he ran home and sneaked his father's gun out of the house. My eyes bugged when I examined the weapon, a richly engraved high-quality English twelve-bore. The tiger-stripe walnut stock glowed with years of loving care.

Buddy loaded up. We watched fearfully as he skated out towards the largest flock. Slowly the gun came up to his skinny little shoulder. He came to a halt and fired. In a fraction of a second his skates were where his head should have been. He came down with an awful crack, knocking himself unconscious. The gun spun across the ice like a thrown ski. Turmoil in the duck pond. Carlo slithered out to retrieve and watched in confusion as every last terrified bird made its frantic escape. Buddy had missed them all.

We carried him ashore. He revived in minute or two and with exploring fingers touched the lump on his skull.

"I was too close," he said gloomily. "Fired both barrels at once. My God, what a kick that thing has. The gun's a mess. My old man will kill me."

"No he won't," said Ernie, handing me the gun. "You're the expert. Will you take care of this?"

So I thoroughly cleaned and polished the gun and Buddy

replaced it in its cabinet. Buddy's father never knew what had happened, and I had the pleasure of working on a Holland and Holland shotgun.

The following summer we went on a good hike. Took up the whole weekend. I bullied my Model T into life, we went through our pockets to find enough money to have the gas tank filled, and away we went to Harrison Mills. We parked the Ford in a logging camp beside the highway and shouldered our packs. With Carlo exploring ahead, we struck out along an old railway gradient that was thickly overgrown with young alder. It was a pleasant hike despite the August heat. Pausing at two lakes, we caught a few trout, some of them coloured a really beautiful green.

We estimated the round trip at eighteen to twenty miles, but Carlo must have covered at least ten times that distance. He charged through the brush up the steep mountainside in search of who knows what, or explored downhill on the other side of the trail. His curiosity almost got him into trouble. We heard one yelp of fear and the next minute he was cowering in our midst.

We thought we knew what had happened. He had probably seen or scented a cougar. We knew that cougars hate dogs and kill them at any opportunity. We were also aware that if a dog gets a chance he will run to his master for protection. We feared for our own safety as much as Carlo's, knowing that if there was a fight the dog would be killed and we could be severely, perhaps fatally, clawed.

We formed a circle, yelling like mad and throwing stones into the bush. The cougar never showed, and when Carlo had calmed down we moved on. The dog stayed close to us for half an hour and then left to explore on his own.

The stream we camped beside that evening made happy

sounds like children's laughter in the distance. We ate an enormous supper of canned beef stew washed down with Ernie's corrosive tea. Darkness came unobtrusively and with a quiet so all-encompassing it seemed as if we could almost reach out and stroke it. There were no night-prowling animals, no owl calls, nothing. Even the banked fire whispered its way through stacked fir bark. Carlo stretched out in a sleep of total exhaustion. We had no tent. Each of us carried a ground sheet and blanket, and that was plenty good enough.

We got home late Sunday night, and Carlo needed several days to recover from our hike. Though young and strong, he had overdone it. For a while, every movement brought a yelp of pain as sore, protesting muscles made their presence known.

A few weeks later some Swedish friends from Toba Inlet arrived with a fresh grizzly hide. We stretched it out on the front room floor. The room was small, about twelve feet square, with a bookcase taking up the entire east wall. That bear hide stretched from the book shelves, and the enormous head filled the doorway. The fur was inches long and a rich chocolate brown. I was shocked by the lifeless hide. To me that bear had been a magnificent animal and should have been left alone, but minding my manners I said nothing.

Carlo trotted in to investigate. Not thinking too clearly he walked onto the hide, inhaled one deep breath, and took off at the speed of a bullet. We heard the screen door give way. I ran after him, noted the spaniel-sized hole in the door, and found him leaning against the back fence, shivering in terror. It took a lot of coaxing to get him back into the house, and still more to get him close to the grizzly. We left him cautiously circling it while we went to the kitchen for lunch. When we returned, Carlo was sleeping peacefully in the middle of the hide.

One winter night, with a sou'easter yowling around the

eaves and the rain threatening to cave in the roof, we heard a piteous mewing at the back door. I opened the door and a sodden cat drooped in. We dried the cat with old towels and fed it. It was a beautiful young tom, lean and graceful and black as polished coal. Carlo hated it instantly.

That cat took over the household. It began by usurping Carlo's hooked rug in the middle of the kitchen floor. Attempts at repossession earned him a scratched nose. Carlo solved the problem in his own way. He would creep up to the kitchen door and, without warning, race past the sleeping cat, letting out one loud bark as he passed by. The cat would spring straight up, every hair on end, as if prodded with an electric cattle goad. Waiting until the cat had gone back to sleep, Carlo would make his barking charge from the opposite direction. Every time, the cat soared ceilingwards in a most satisfying manner. Two weeks of that kind of treatment left the cat a nervous wreck. It just up and left one rainy day. We never saw it again.

Carlo was our constant companion for a long time. He hiked with us, hunted with us, and loved car riding. He has been gone many years, but I have not owned a dog since. Parting is not sweet sorrow. It's just sorrow.

THE
WILD
BLUE
YONDER
BOYS

*B*efore Mr. Dougherty sold a portion of his Sea Island farm to the government for an international airport, there was an airfield on Lulu Island. It was just that, a field, nothing more, where cows roamed at will along with hordes of interested spectators. Landing an aircraft under those conditions ranked high among the hazardous occupations.

Many were the picturesque old kites which we, as teenagers, assured each other were the ultimate in airplane design. We talked learnedly about airfoil section, dihedral angle, and the advantages of monoplane design as we studied the de Havilland Moth and the vast, ungainly Ford Tri-Motor, and wondered at the tip-tilted wings of the Barling NB3. There was even a Golden Eagle powered by a three-cylinder, ninety-horsepower Le Blond engine. Ninety horsepower in that little thing! Wow!

One Sunday Gabby, Ernie, and I along with Torchy—who was a scientific thinker and knew all there was to know about aircraft—mingled with the crowd staring at the massive Ford Tri-Motor standing there, a giant hawk among the dragon flies, with all engines idling slowly.

We watched as a man, obviously a farmhand, climbed into the Ford. Then, to our collective horror, the starboard engine opened up with a terrifying roar, the stubble jumper hit the ground on the run, and the huge plane spun around and headed in an arc for a number of small aircraft parked nearby. The monster bore down on an innocent little de Havilland Moth, seemingly in hate. Flying wreckage filled the air as the Ford's three-bladed metal prop, whirling like a giant meat cutter, ate its way along the entire length of the Moth's wing and into the fusilage before a mechanic scrambled into the machine and shut off the engine. We could see the farmhand in the distance, still running.

With all this interest in aircraft it was inevitable that we should attempt to build one. Not a power-driven affair, since our collective finances could not possibly cope with that, but a relatively simple, inexpensive glider. At least it seemed simple enough, as we studied the plan Torchy had discovered in an old copy of *Popular Mechanics*. Building it was something else entirely. Much of the material was hard to come by. We required waterproof glue, an all-but-unknown commodity in those days, and hardware merchants looked askance when we asked for a hundred feet of aileron control cable.

To begin with, we had to clear a vacant lot next door to Gabby's home and erect a shed, all of which took considerable time. Torchy took charge of the operation and delegated jobs. Ernie, the expert scrounger, became the buyer. Gabby and his brother Torchy did most of the actual construction. A friend named Jack, who later became a mechanic for Ginger Cootes, the famous bush pilot, did all the rigging. Having but little aptitude for and, at best, only a tepid interest in things mechanical, I was left to do the odd jobs, especially the awkward ones beyond the physical reach of my average-sized companions.

When we had completed the glider's framework to Torchy's satisfaction, we covered it with well-stretched, unbleached muslin and gave it several coats of orange shellac to shrink and toughen the fabric. It looked hideous. The fabric buckled and rippled between the frames in a revolting fashion—it looked like an alligator with a skin disease—but there was nothing we could do about it.

At last the great day came for the first test flight. We met at the building shed long before daybreak, picked up the glider, and carried it half a mile to a spot where the City Fathers, in their wisdom, had constructed an excellent concrete road across an open field.

With the first hint of daylight Torchy sat at the controls, Gabby attached the towline to Jack's Model T, Torchy waved a signal to go ahead, and away they went, wings rocking perilously and sparks showering off the keel. The glider did not become airborne and it was obvious that the keel would not tolerate much more of the grindstone treatment.

We moved the whole outfit into the field, where the Model T had difficulty getting traction on the wet grass. After a time the sun evaporated the dew, and Jack's Ford lurched away with the glider bouncing up and down behind it like a demented grasshopper. When Torchy finally became airborne he sailed for some fifty yards, side-slipping dangerously, then landed with a thump that snapped off the tail assembly.

We concluded that the glider was too heavy and lacked balance. Jack's old car had not had sufficient power to tow the sailplane fast enough for it to become properly airborne. Whether our theories were correct or not is of no consequence. For a brief moment our Torchy had soared like an eagle, and that was important.

THE REMITTANCE MAN

*W*hen Gabby, Ernie, and I reached the age where we left school to go to work, we and the Depression made our debuts simultaneously. Gabby worked in sawmills. Ernie was an office man. I started out as a commerical artist and ended up a seaman.

Few people managed to gain employment they were really suited for, and anyone with an aptitude for the arts was plain out of luck. Logging, mining, farming, and commercial fishing were the chief occupations.

Newcomers to the labour market were faced with a number of serious problems, not the least of which was the pre-dominance of certain nationalities in industry and municipal and governmental departments. Most loggers were Scandinavians. The Japanese dominated commercial fishing, that is, the salmon gillnetting end of it. Sawmills employed large numbers of East Indians and Chinese. In Vancouver, Highland Scots predominated in the police force, the parks department, and, to a large measure, the fire department. In Victoria the legislative buildings were full of civil servants straight out from England. We who had just left school had no opportunity to get into anything unless we were lucky enough to know someone with influence. There was no proper apprenticeship system. So-called apprentices were hired as cheap labour and nothing more. With some bitterness we told each other that the most heinous crime anyone could commit was to be born a native Canadian.

There was one group of men who had been around for a long time and who bothered no one. They were the retired British Army types, frequently Indian Army, scions of ancient families, who had left home willingly or otherwise. Because they lived on small pensions or on donations from aristocratic families, Canadians referred to them as "remittance men."

They were largely ignored, and often looked upon as a collection of lazy bums. Nothing could have been further from the truth. When a man has served twenty-five or thirty years in the army, especially "where the heat would make your bloomin' eyebrows crawl," he is entitled to a rest in a decent climate. Those who lived on the money from home were here for an infinite number of reasons. There were some, no doubt, who could not face a life of starched shirts and tea at precisely four o'clock. Others had besmirched the family escutcheon by dating the downstairs maid or simply by confessing to a loathing for cucumber sandwiches.

Superb manners, unfailing courtesy, and superior education were their common characteristics. Remittance men often filled a void left by Canadians whose schooling had been abruptly terminated by the necessity to go to work. If a legal letter needed to be written, a language needed to be translated, or a question on international politics needed to be answered, these men could do it. They could be relied upon to start a library, coach a drama group, or teach any of the creative arts. If a community needed someone to conduct a class in fencing, wing shooting, or fly fishing, then some drawling Oxonian would stroll in and take over.

We three got to know several remittance men. I travelled more than my friends, up and down the coast and on Vancouver Island, and so became acquainted with quite a number of them.

In Vancouver and Victoria the retired army personnel often joined the Corps of Commissionaires. They were especially valuable in Vancouver's polyglot population. Some of them understood three or four European languages, and others spoke Semitic languages or Chinese. I remember one commissionaire chatting Swahili to a black seaman from Durban, South Africa.

There was a man on duty every Saturday at a large down-town department store. He knew where everything was and directed customers with style. With a back straight as a rifle barrel, a clipped grey moustache, and five rows of medal ribbons, he looked exactly what he was: a gentleman and a fine old soldier. We liked him a lot.

One Saturday sale day we three strolled into the store. We had no money to spend, but this was one place to while away a rainy day. Our friend was directing human traffic at the foot of a double stairway. A large sign read "Please Keep to the Right." Perhaps because of an inability to read English, a group of East Indian women started up the left staircase, causing a traffic jam. Our uniformed friend spoke to them courteously.

"Keep to the right, please, ladies."

They ignored him and continued shoving into the crowd. Calm, unruffled, without a change of expression, the old soldier let rip a stream of Punjabi. We had never seen women move so fast. In an instant they had changed course and headed up the right stairway. Our friend gave us a sly wink.

There were retired military men from every colony, man-date, and protectorate. Some were as quiet and reserved as hermits. Others were talkative, and enjoyed nothing more than wedging someone into a corner and delivering long orations on the habits of the Cape buffalo, the proper way to make a gin pahit, or how to shoot crocodiles on the Hooghly. If there was no escape, one kept quiet and learned a lot.

One old boy talked at some length about the time when the expression "the natives were friendly" was more than a cliché. In Burma, in the Malay States, and especially in Africa, unfriendly natives had a way of expressing their resentment to white superiority with accurately thrown spears. To be a police commissionaire anywhere in British Africa called for a special type of man—more accurately, two types. One was the hard, tough-minded brute who lived by the book and made no effort to understand the people under his control. He survived as long as his bodyguard remained loyal. Fortunately, such officers were few and far between.

The other type had a built-in sense of fair play. He dispensed justice impartially, relying more on common sense than on the letter of the law. He lived with the people under his jurisdiction, spoke their language, and ate their food. But most important, he was a good listener, and therein lay his strength and popularity.

Our friend Major Charles Fairchild was such a man. When the Boer War ended, he and his wife moved to Africa, where he administered the law over some five thousand square miles of bush and veldt. Initiation into this experience must have been traumatic for Mrs. Fairchild. At home in England she had been surrounded by tradition and protection. She not only survived Africa for nearly thirty years, but also came to love it, and left with regret when her husband retired to move to B.C.

Because of her husband's position, Mrs. Fairchild had become accustomed to even more servants in Africa than she had known at home. She never learned to be a housekeeper. Her accomplishments as a cook still began and ended with pouring boiling water into a teapot. The Major was equally hopeless as a handyman. They were the last people in the world who should own a resort. Yet in 1932, they bought an overpriced collection of run-down log cabins by a lake, and went into business.

Gabby, Ernie, and I met them after they had been in business a few weeks. We had been fishing the lake and had caught our limit of cutthroat trout. On our way back to the car, a slight man of medium height stopped us with a friendly gesture. He explained almost diffidently that we were trespassing on private property. We apologized, saying we did not realize that the place was occupied. We offered him some trout.

"Awfully decent of you chaps," he said, "but we don't know how to clean them, actually."

"Don't worry," we assured him. "They're cleaned."

"But we don't know how to cook them."

That seemed a bit much. Ernie had become a good camp cook by this time. After but a moment's hesitation he offered to give a demonstration of trout frying.

"Jolly good notion," the man said. "Name's Fairchild, by the way. Major of sorts. Come along. Wife will make tea."

The afternoon had turned chilly. The thin column of smoke from the stone chimney spoke of warmth within. The major opened the door. Smoke billowed out. For an awful moment we thought the place was on fire, until a cheerful voice bade us enter. We advanced through the gloom and I tripped over a log.

"Don't have saws, axes, things like that," the major explained. "Wouldn't know how to use them anyway. We simply drag in a great lump of wood and shove the end into the fireplace. Fire travels underneath sometimes. Smokes up the place a bit."

Without further discussion we three picked up the log and carried it outside to a patch of gravel. We left it smouldering while we attacked various stumps with our belt axes. We packed in armloads of bark, and soon had a fire blazing in the fireplace. The major opened the doors and windows.

There was no cook stove, but the fireplace was fitted out with a series of hobs. Ernie made a good job of the trout. We drank excellent tea. In an hour we felt as if we had known the Fairchilds all our lives. We were relaxing and enjoying ourselves when the major startled us by suddenly springing up to his feet.

"Good God," he exclaimed. "Almost forgot. Time to feed the guests."

He shot out of the cabin. We heard the roar of a motor and the clatter of spraying gravel rattling against the log wall.

"We have five paying guests here for the fishing," Mrs. Fairchild explained in a perfectly unruffled voice. "We foolishly advertised cabins with meals, thinking that cooking would be easy enough. It wasn't, as we found out. Cookbooks are far more complicated than chemistry textbooks. Charles nips into the village and buys roast beef, vegetables, and so forth that the hotel cooks for us, then rushes back with it."

The village was fourteen miles away. We were afraid to ask how the meals were supposed to keep hot or survive Charles's driving over miles of potholes.

We visited the Fairchilds whenever we could, which was not often enough. We learned all about policing the wilds of Africa. On one occasion we demonstrated the use and abuse of a double-bitted axe, and conveniently forgot to take it away with us. Our friends never learned to cook or repair anything. In a year they had sold out and moved to Victoria, where Major Fairchild was determined to write a book on his African experiences. He never did, though, or at least we never heard of it.

It was not always easy to identify a remittance man. One chap baffled us for years. He travelled under the unlovely sobriquet of Conky Timber Jones, but everyone addressed him as Conky. He was a hand logger who worked alone. That was unusual. Hand logging was usually done by a two-man team. It was a hazardous and generally wasteful occupation whose practitioners needed only a large rowboat, an axe or two, a falling saw, a couple of wedges, and a Gilchrist jack. One partner would spot a good fir or cedar close to the water. He would then climb the usual rock face to his tree and study the problem. If he decided that the tree could be felled and the logs rolled into the salt chuck, he would call to his mate to pack up some needed equipment. If a log hung up, the Gilchrist jack would usually push it over the edge. Sometimes the men would limb a tree and buck it in the water.

A great many men tried hand logging, and failed. Conky Timber Jones was an expert. Three or four times a year he would assemble a sizable boom and sell it to a log buyer. With a pocket full of money Jones would head for Vancouver and a two-week spree. We met him often, cheerfully drunk and bothering no one. Sometimes he would talk to us about the world and its affairs in un-logger-like terminology that betrayed a vast knowledge of the English language. On one occasion he dropped a hint about his background.

"Spent all my money, chaps. Never mind. Expecting a cheque from home in a day or two."

I signed on as deckhand on a coastal passenger-freighter. Conky Timber Jones appeared one morning southbound for Vancouver. He was grubby, unshaven, and ragged, but cheerful. A fortnight later he staggered aboard in an ugly black temper to match his hangover. He had a new suit with the trousers stumped off level with the tops of new spiked boots, "caulk shoes" the loggers called them. He barged into the dining saloon, demanding service. The steward did his level best, but nothing suited Jones. Conky ended his performance by jumping up and down on the table, yelling and kicking dishes.

Someone told me that this ridiculous behaviour had been going on for years. The company would send Jones a bill for damages, which he paid without a murmur.

We had a student deckhand taking a year off from theological college to bolster his bank account and learn more about people. He met Conky Timber Jones. The two men hit it off instantly. When the student mentioned his ambition to become a clergyman, Jones made a wry face. A discussion started and Jones's logger's slang gradually disappeared as he warmed to his subject. He talked at length on Buddhism, Shinto, Islam, and Christianity. The student asked endless questions. Conky gave answers in an increasingly polished Cambridge accent.

This sort of discussion went on whenever possible during the four-day voyage. The rest of us listened in whenever we could. The student wrote page after page of notes. He admitted to learning more about theology during those four days than in three years of college. In fact, he told us, he had learned so much that he had decided to switch to social service work.

Who was Conky Timber Jones? The question nagged at our minds and caused much argument. What was his real name? Was he an unfrocked parson or just someone who preferred the raw Canadian wilderness to the orderly English countryside? What would motivate a man of his background to give up a life of peaceful ease for a series of binges between months of backbreaking labour? We never settled the argument, nor did we ever have the opportunity to ask Conky outright. We never saw him again after that voyage. He just up and vanished.

Remittance men. There were some phonies, of course, especially among the retired soldiery. Not a few promoted themselves a rank or two. I suppose that "colonel" has a nicer ring to it than "captain," but why bother? We natives liked a man or did not like him. "The rank is but the guinea's stamp; the man's the gold for a' that."

There was a character we knew who lived in a small Vancouver Island town. A World War I veteran with a swagger stick tucked under his arm, he stalked about the town at one hundred and forty paces per minute exactly. He had prominent glassy blue eyes and a waxed moustache so precisely trimmed he must have measured it with a micrometer. He never spoke unless spoken to first. No one dared to omit his rank.

"Morning, Major."

"Mornin', Sah." A cryptic bark.

As the years passed the major grew cantankerous. He refused to give an inch on a crowded sidewalk. He made a nuisance of himself at Canadian Legion meetings, barking at everybody. World War II came and went, and the new veterans straggled home. One of them decided to check into the major's record. It took a few weeks of letter-writing to dredge up a startling fact. In reality the "major" had actually been a sergeant major, and a mere company sergeant major at that. News travels quickly in a small town. In an hour or two everyone was greeting the "major" with "Morning, Sergeant Major." He left town in a few days, never to be seen again.

In my thinking, it was cruel to prick such a harmless bubble. The old guy had admittedly lived a lie, but had never bothered anyone seriously.

There are few, if any, real remittance men around any more. They arrived, lived somewhat eccentric lives, and passed on. But they left their mark, and those of us who knew them remember them with pleasure.

SMUGGLERS
THREE

*T*he chilly night mists of autumn hung low over Sea Island and the Fraser and the bullrush swamps that bordered the river. Groping our way through the fog, we three young fellows rowed our heavy, flat-bottomed skiff towards the mud bank at the foot of Angus Drive. Ernie, kneeling on a sack of potatoes in the bow, peered into the enveloping white and gave whispered commands. Gabby and I rowed cautiously, feathering the oars with nary a splash.

During the early thirties, the potato marketing board imposed a twenty-five cent tax on every sack of spuds that was hauled from Lulu and Sea Islands to the downtown wholesale warehouse. The reason for this act is obscure. We never did see any sense in taxing foodstuffs, but then, we were not alone in our inability to understand the weird ways of government.

The farmers, as usual, were the people who suffered. They were barely eking out a living anyway, even from the rich alluvial soil of the Fraser River islands, and a two-bit tag on every hundred pounds of potatoes could mean the difference between profit and loss.

In those days there were only two bridges in a direct line with downtown Vancouver: at Marpole and at Fraser streets. Anyone attempting to truck potatoes across those bridges had to stop for inspection or else run the gauntlet of provincial policemen.

The provincial force had recruited special policemen for the inspection, and one of them stationed on the Marpole bridge ran into trouble. A Chinese gardener rolled up at his customary speed of eight miles an hour and neglected to stop at the checkpoint. The young special jumped onto the running board and grabbed the steering wheel. The gardener bit the policeman's hand severely, stomped on the accelerator, and raced across the bridge at a speed his aged truck had never before attempted. Got away with it, too.

The farmers grumbled a good deal. A few of them proclaimed that they would sooner let their spuds rot in the ground than bow down to Caesar. One of them, who shall be nameless, made us a proposition. He offered us, for free, all the potatoes we could dig, sack, and transport across the river. He promised to arrange with a Chinese wholesaler to meet us in the dead of night to pick up the contraband.

So we dug by day and rowed by night. Digging and sacking were not particularly difficult, even in the Sea Island mud. However, to shoulder a sack and hike across fields, over fences, across roads and dikes, to conceal the booty in the willows and wild rose thickets at the river's edge was something else. It is surprising how a load which starts out at a hundred pounds can gain weight. We prepared one cargo at a time, six sacks, and even at that the boat was seriously overloaded with the three of us aboard as well. On fine nights we stayed home. Being students of Dr. Syn of Romney Marsh, we knew the perils of smuggling at times other than the dark of the moon or when the fog was thick.

The Chinese wholesaler always met us at a pre-arranged time and paid cash, a dollar a sack. We were making money hand over fist: upwards of fifteen cents an hour, near as we could figure. We would load our friend's pickup, collect our money, and watch him drive away with his lights out until he reached Marine Drive.

One night we nearly met our doom. Hidden by the mist, we rowed across the river. By this time we were so used to the route that we had no difficulty locating our landing place in the bullrushes. With the sensitive hearing of youth we noticed something in the reeds—a faint rustle, furtive as a muskrat—that put us on the alert. We rested on the oars, listening. There were other sounds, and a strange, unnatural movement coming from several directions in the swamp. Hijackers? Unlikely. Who would bother with a few sacks of spuds worth a dollar each? Police? More than likely. We backed noiselessly out into the stream and slowly eased our cargo over the gunwales, a sack at a time. When the last sack had slipped silently into the river, we rowed to our harbour on Jimmie's Island and hid our boat. We crossed the island and made our way over the cedar log booms, no easy task in the fog, to Hunting and Merritt's shingle mill, and from there on home.

We telephoned our Chinese friend, who called off all further smuggling. He hinted that he had barely escaped arrest himself on that memorable night.

A few weeks later the marketing board removed the potato tax, probably because of the trouble and expense of trying to enforce such an unpopular law. With that, the lives of the smugglers three returned to a humdrum, unexciting norm.

FISH
SHOOTING
AND
OTHER
FOOLISHNESS

*W*e nicknamed him the Mad Butcher. We, the inseparable three, had been on a hunting trip to Cowichan Lake one autumn and the butcher had kindly given us a lift from Youbou to Duncan. What a wild ride that was at fifty miles an hour over a gravel road with just enough surface remaining to separate the pot holes. The butcher, middle European with curly black hair, a broad, smiling face and laughter in his voice, owned a shop in Youbou and made all the twice-weekly deliveries himself. Since his route covered somewhere close to a hundred and fifty miles he found it imperative to cover it with all possible speed. At every crossroad or railway track he had marked an escape route to avoid collision.

"You vatch," he yelled happily, "I coming to road. Maybe trock coming hit me. No! I torn fast, bust t'rough dat gate into yard. Oh, boy! Got to be smart drive dis road. Busted two spring dis veek. Not bad. Busted t'ree las' veek. Now I coming railvay track. Is coming train I dive into hardack svamp. No hort me. No hort trock. Smart, hey?"

We hung on, hoping for the best, hurtling down the mountain road. We debarked at Duncan where our marvellous mad butcher waved a cheerful hand and whizzed away before we could so much as say thank you.

After a much needed shower and shave at the Tzouhalem Hotel we settled back to review our safari, and decide upon the best way to transport knapsacks, firearms, and the modest products of our hunt to Vancouver. One thing was certain. Whatever decision we reached the trip could only end up as hard work.

Two weeks previously Gabby, Ernie, and I had left Vancouver via the CPR ferry to Nanaimo. A bus to Duncan and another to the little village of Lake Cowichan left us with he problem of getting out into the bush. A logger whom we questioned promptly arranged passage for us on a logging train headed for who knows where. He told the engineer to let us off at "old number nine married quarters," whatever that meant.

Number nine married quarters, where a fireman wordlessly handed down our packs and shooting irons, turned out to be a collection of run-down deserted shacks rising out of the alder and willow that had begun to cover the logged-off land. We looked over the cabins, selected on which appeared to have the soundest roof and smelled less strongly of mice than the rest, and settled in.

One day, while Gabby was off somewhere exploring on his own, Ernie and I followed the railway track to a low bridge crossing an unusual creek. On the south side of the bridge the stream ran only inches deep over water-polished stones. On the other side was a wide pool we estimated to be twelve or fifteen feet deep. The bottom was covered with enormous fish resting in straight lines like troops on parade.

We always carried tackle of sorts with us: a light handline, a few snelled hooks, small spinners and such. Every lure in the box was tested without result. Hooks loaded with preserved salmon roe were dangled in front of their noses only to be ignored. Finally, one fish broke ranks and swam to the surface. We wondered why, until we saw the floating yellow huckleberry leaf which had attracted the steelhead's attention. I whipped out a Stevens single shot .22 pistol, a weapon of fair accuracy despite the heavy trigger pull, and shot the fish through the head just as it broke water.

All hell broke loose. The dying fish thrashed its way out of the pool into the fast-running shallows. Ernie leapt off the bridge and scooped the thing up in his arms. Wet, blood-spattered and triumphant, he scrambled up the gravel bank clutching the still struggling trout.

We had no way of weighing that fish. It was heavy and long. I'm well over six feet and as I stood with my arms straight in front and with my fingers in the gills, the tail dragged on the ground. Only three thick steaks were eaten and then we'd had enough. The remainder was left out in the woods in the hope that a bear or a raccoon might find it. Something did enjoy a free meal, evidently, because it was gone the next day.

It had been an altogether successful vacation. Even our journey from Duncan to Nanaimo was arranged for us. A logger we met insisted upon taking us, our equipment, and two deer in his truck, making the offhand comment that he was going that way anyhow. We learned a fact of life that trip which has proven correct many times since. If you want a helping hand ask a logger. Rough, tough men they were, who often lived and worked under deplorable conditions which they accepted as their way of life and let it go at that. Given to hard drinking and bare-knuckle fighting, they cruised more timber and felled more trees in the beer parlour than they did out in the woods. They were generous with their time and money and usually ended up in an early grave or in a skidroad hotel, their energies burnt out by overwork and too much booze. Great guys, those old-time loggers.

On our way home we managed, with our usual skill, to shatter the dignity of that oak panelled, glass doorknobbed pride of the CPR coastal fleet, S.S. *Princess Elaine*.

A brass-buttoned official had overruled our request to take our guns with us into the saloon and insisted that we leave them with our other belongings on the freight deck. We were afraid of theft. Money was too hard to come by, and firearms have always been expensive.

As we strolled the deck, fuming impotently, we found a small tin of yellow paint and a brush. Then we remembered the notice painted on a certain door: GENTLEMEN, and beheath that, STEP OVER DOOR SILL. With the addition of one letter and a comma we changed all that—

GENTLEMEN
STEP OVER DOOR, SILLY

The red-faced gent with the zigzag stripes on his sleeves didn't think much of it.

OLD
PAT

*T*o the south of Cultus Lake the land rises sharply to an almost level plateau. The area is cut by deep ravines and was, at the time of my story, a blackened scar where sprouting willows and alders were just beginning to camouflage the hideous devastation left by the worst forest fire in the area's history. And Old Pat had started it.

Three or four years before the fire, Pat had retired with a constable's rank after a lifetime in the RCMP. He had saved no money, owned nothing, and found that his monthly pension of twenty-eight dollars could not sustain him above the poverty level, even during the hungry thirties. He repaired to Cultus Lake and, without bothering to stake a claim, moved into the woods with the intention of making his home there. The land was one vast forest of Douglas fir and cedar. In the swamps hundreds of deer browsed, and in every stream rainbow and cutthroat trout were there for the taking.

Arriving too late in the fall to attempt building a shanty, Pat moved his few belongings into a cedar snag that had been burned out by a forest fire at least a century before. He made a crude thatched roof from strips of cedar bark that kept out most of the rain, and fashioned a fire pit close at hand.

His first winter was almost his last. Bears ate his supplies and pack rats stole his socks. Hungry almost to the point of starvation, he trudged fifteen miles to the nearest store, bought as much food as he could afford, and hiked back after resting a few days in an abandoned cabin.

In the spring his explorations led him to a natural meadow, thick with dead bracken. He cleared a suitable space and built a pole and cedar shake cabin. His next project was to make a place for his garden. Without considering the possible consequences, he simply set fire to the bracken, which was so dry that it literally exploded. The blaze quickly caught the surrounding forest, and, in a holocaust which ended two miles across the border in Washington State, destroyed a million acres of prime timber. Somehow, Old Pat and his cabin survived.

The old man's cabin became headquarters for Gabby, Ernie, and me when we hunted that part of the province. Seated around his rusty kitchen range, we listened to his gleeful description of how he had started the great forest fire. It was the one big accomplishment of his life. We slept in the cabin only once, and rose at dawn heavy-eyed and flea-bitten. After that we bedded down out-of-doors, preferring to take our chances with the weather.

Have you ever heard a cougar scream? It is an impressive sound, especially at night when you are hiking along a barely visible trail a hundred miles from nowhere and black clouds are racing across the bright harvest moon. Every rustle becomes the approach of the hunting cat, every dimly seen log a crouching cougar. Mountain lions seldom tangle with people, but a cat will attack a man if it is hungry enough, or rendered too slow by old age or injury to catch deer. Aware of this, we kept close together with rifles at the ready, and were very relieved when we arrived at Old Pat's cabin.

We drank coffee from scantily washed mugs as we discussed the screaming cougar with our host. Pat was not impressed.

"Them animals is the darndest cowards in the woods," he stated. "Run from anybody. I seen tracks in the garden this morning. You boys going to sleep outside?"

We told him that this was our intention, since we had his assurance that a cougar was nothing to fear. We diplomatically refrained from mentioning his flea-infested mattresses.

Having spread ground sheets and blankets under a tarpaulin lashed to a rail fence, we turned in. Around midnight I awakened, alerted by a sense of danger, and looked around as best I could without moving. The clouds had gone, the moon was up, and in the pool of soft light a cougar crouched, tail lashing slowly, not thirty feet away. I carefully eased my rifle out of my bed, then realized that the big cat was not interested in us. It was staring fixedly at Old Pat's mongrel spaniel, who leaned shivering against the fence.

I sat up cautiously and attempted to draw a bead at the point where the cougar's neck met its hunched shoulders, but in spite of the bright moonlight, it was impossible to see the sights properly. I was aware how dangerous a wounded carnivore can be, and knew that this was a one-shot, shoot-to-kill opportunity. I tried desperately to take a proper aim, and finally had it. Just as I was about to squeeze the trigger, the cabin door burst open and Old Pat rushed out, snatched up a garden hoe, and charged, yelling like a demon, straight for the cougar. Gabby and Ernie sat bolt upright, just in time to see the last of the cat bounding into the bush.

"I told you them animals was cowards," said Old Pat, hugging his dog. "Nothing to worry about. C'mon, you dumb mutt, let's go in the cabin."

MODEL
T
BLUES

It was Tin, Tin, Tin,
You limping heap of hardware, Hunka Tin,
I've cursed you and I've flayed you,
But by Henry Ford that made you,
You're better than the Packard, Hunka Tin.

*T*hat travesty on Mr. Kipling's classic was running through my head while I adjusted the transmission bands in my Model T's oily interior. What those bands actually did, what their function was, has never been clear to me. All I knew was that they were a diabolical invention which had to be kept tight, but not too tight. When they wore out and had to be replaced, it was easy to remove them. It was necessary only to take out the pedal-attached crossbolt, coil spring, and angle plates that held the band together, grab one end, and pull lustily. The band sprang out, showering oil. Getting a new band into place was something else. Made of thin spring steel with a strip of thick canvas riveted onto it, the band was poked into a cast iron transmission case cunningly designed so that even the smallest hand could not reach inside. The usual solution to that problem was to tie a length of baling wire onto the band and feed it around the drum first. When the band was more or less in place, you would hold it together with one hand and insert the crossbolt, coil spring, and locking lugs with the other. Hah! A very pretty theory. The bits and pieces always leapt out of oily fingers and plunked irretrievably into the transmission case.

How a Model T mechanism worked I have no idea. Torchy said it was a simple epicyclic system involving three sets of planetary gears revolving within a rotating annulus. Bully for you, Torchy. You were no help to me. All I know is that there were three pedals protruding from the floorboards and connected to the bands for some obscure reason. When you shoved down the left pedal the machine was in low gear. Fully released it was in high gear. The middle position, found entirely by feel, was neutral. You pressed down the middle pedal for reverse and the right one for the brake. It would have been convenient to have three feet.

It would also have been convenient to have three hands or, better still, four—two for steering and two for operating the gas and spark levers. These levers stuck out at an angle under the steering wheel. The one on the right was the throttle. To start out on a journey, you cranked the motor into life and sprang into the seat before the motor stalled. To warm up the engine, you advanced the gas and spark controls a little. When the motor sounded about right and the car body was vibrating comfortingly, you placed your left foot on the gear pedal and released the emergency brake. Slight pressure on the foot indicated that the transmission was in neutral. So far, so good.

The next step was fully as difficult as patting the head and rubbing the stomach at the same time. Advance spark and throttle. Push pedal into low gear and hold to ten miles an hour, more or less. This was pure guesswork. The Model T had no speedometer. Next, close spark and throttle, let the foot off the pedal to engage high gear, and quickly advance spark and throttle. While all this was going on, it was also essential to steer the vehicle. You became accustomed to these manoeuvres after a while, but a T Model takeoff always resembled a knock-down, drag-out fight between owner and car.

Reversing was a chancy business. Depress left pedal to neutral position, shove in middle pedal, mess about with gas and spark and hope for the best. The Ford either juddered backwards with dignity and aplomb, or else took off like one of the more successful rocket launchings. It all depended upon how tight the bands were.

Braking was relatively easy. Find neutral and stomp on the brake pedal. You used reverse if the brake was not working too well. That stopped the old beast.

Well, anyhow, I got the bands tightened properly. Time for a test run. I fitted a piece of wood between the seat and the Ruckstell axle lever to keep it in neutral. Then I took a good grip on the crank handle and with my left hand pulled on a bit of wire that protruded from the radiator and closed the choke. I cranked a few turns and released the choke wire. I cranked again. And again. I cranked until my arm was numb. Fatigued, thirsty, and furious, I dealt the radiator a vicious kick and cranked anew. No go. Wiping the sweat out of my eyes, I decided I had had enough. I released the brake and walked around to the back end. Bracing both feet and giving one good heave, I got the car moving.

My plan was simple and murderous. If I could get the Ford to the corner, I could coast a mile to the dump and dispose of my troubles once and for all. So I pushed. I had to conquer a slight grade before making the street corner, and that beat me. Just then my friend Max came along.

"What do you think you're doing?"

"I'm heading for the dump, that's what I'm doing," I replied, somewhat irate. "Help me push this blasted thing."

Instead, Max walked around to the front and pushed against me. Recognizing defeat, I helped him get the Ford back into my yard.

"What now?" I wanted to know.

"Patience," he said. "Wait here while I hike home for some tools."

Max was a great mechanic. He had patience and knowledge.

He could repair anything and tune a racing motorbike to perfection. Max worked the rest of the day on the old heap. When he had finished, it probably ran better than it did when it was new.

Cold-weather starting was quite a performance. You always had to drain the radiator at night to prevent freezing. To buy antifreeze was economically unsound, because Model T radiators had a nasty habit of developing leaks. The first chore, therefore, was to close the radiator petcock and fill the radiator with boiling water. As a precautionary measure, one rear wheel was jacked up clear of the ground, or the Ruckstell axle, if there was one, was pushed into neutral. All of this was really necessary. Coated with oil the bands would not release until the whole unit was hot. The vehicle was in gear, so to speak. Many an owner was injured on a cold day when he started his motor and his car ran into him. One sure way to get a broken arm was to have the crank kick back because the spark was too far advanced.

High-pressure tires were famous for resounding blowouts— usually at night in the pouring rain. A spare tire was carried as a matter of course but was seldom mounted and ready on a spare rim. Getting a tire onto a rim was no quick change operation. The four locking nuts were backed off while the car swayed on a jack that always seemed to find soft ground to rest on. With the rim removed and the shattered tire ripped off, somehow the replacement was pried into the rim using two tire irons, both hands, both feet, and all the help you could get. Working up forty pounds pressure with a hand pump was no fun either. If one ran over a nail or some sharp object, the tube was repaired with a cold patch. That was anything but reliable. Luckily for us we always carried a hot patch kit some bright inventor had introduced. It worked well. The kit consisted of half a dozen small tins something like half an aspirin box with a rubber patch stuck on the underside. The tin was packed with what looked like brown papier-mâché which was impregnated with an inflammable chemical. The puncture area was carefully cleaned with gasoline and the white backing was stripped from the patch. Next, the whole thing was placed on top of the puncture and held down with a stick or a long spike. Garage men used an efficient clamp for the purpose but of course we never owned such a thing. When the papier-mâché stuff was lighted it fizzed and fumed for a few seconds, emitting a nauseating odor, but it developed enough heat to do a pretty good vulcanizing job. Hurrah for the science and industry combo.

My Ford was equipped with a Ruckstell axle and Rocky Mountain brakes. Often I fervently wished that these mechanisms had never been invented. The Ruckstell was built into the differential and was activated by a lever rearing up through the floorboards. In forward position, it provided a high gear that was almost an overdrive. Hauling the lever back gave a very low, hill-climbing gear. Middle position was neutral. The Ruckstell had one serious and dangerous fault. Occasionally, it would slip out of high gear. When that happened the car was free-wheeling with a vengeance. The rear end was completely disconnected. There were no brakes, no reverse, nothing. Moreover, there was just no way that the Ruckstell could be forced back into gear.

The Rocky Mountain brakes were supposed to stop the vehicle. The name had obviously arisen from some advertising man's fevered imagination. The inference was, of course, that Rocky Mountain brakes would stop a Model T hurtling down a Rocky Mountain. Sure they would, if you collided with the next mountain.

A week or two after Max's repair job my grandmother decided to do a bit of shopping on South Hill, a district on Fraser Street about six miles from home. Grandmother was a remarkable woman. Straight-backed, very proper, and with a classic profile, she never suffered a loss of dignity and never forgot that she was a gentlewoman. She spoke the best English and the most musical French I have ever heard in all my travels. As a young woman she had moved to France just after the Franco-Prussian War of 1870 to teach English, but had ended up teaching French.

It was a fine day. Grandmother shopped; I carried parcels and suffered the boredom common to all grandsons on a shopping tour. When she was finished, we loaded the Ford with assorted merchandise and started for home. At 59th Avenue, just as we broke over the hill, the Ruckstell slipped out of gear. The Ford picked up speed while I fought a losing battle with the Ruckstell. Grandmother sat straight-backed, saying nothing.

We careened down the hill at a speed matched only by the more daring drivers at the Manx Grand Prix. Marine Drive loomed menacingly, busy with cars and trucks. Somehow I steered between them and shot across the flat and over a bridge, finally coasting to a stop on the far side of Mitchell Island. I drooped, shaking, over the steering wheel.

"By jove," said Grandmother, "that was exciting, wasn't it?"

Some claimed that a Model T could wade through two feet of molasses. That was not much of an exaggeration. If you slithered into a snowdrift, getting out of it was a simple feat. You pulled the spark and throttle levers down, revving the motor until it threatened to rise off the frame, and worked the low gear and reverse pedals alternatively to get the car rocking back and forth. This was impossible with a more sophisticated gear system. No one was capable of shifting gears fast enough. When you had the Ford rocking at a good speed, a final yank on the throttle made her leap into the clear. Getting fouled up in a snowdrift was so much fun that we did it deliberately.

One day, about a year after Max had overhauled it, my car let out a wheezing gasp and gave up for good. What to do? Times were tough, and selling it would be difficult. It would not fetch more than ten dollars on the open market. A few blocks from home there was an eight-year-old Rolls Royce for sale for a hundred and fifty bucks, and nobody even bothered to look at it. I decided to dismantle my old beast and sell it piecemeal. Rims and tires sold first. The rest of it gradually disappeared and I realized about thirty-five dollars. I was left with just the body and frame, which I had to get rid of somehow. A vacant lot out back seemed the logical resting place. I tied a heavy rope to the front end and pulled. It was slow work, but I eventually got the carcass out of my yard and across the lane. There I was stymied. I just did not have the strength to roll the body over into the bush. A neighbour turned up.

"Can I give you a hand, kid?"

I looked him up and down. His neck boiled over his collar and a noble frontal development started at his breastbone and extended outward, seemingly forever.

"What can this fat guy do?" I asked myself.

He must have read my mind. Casually brushing me aside with a sweep of his hand, he caught hold of the car and lifted it easily. Under all that fat he must have had the muscles of a gorilla, I thought. Resting the load on his bay window he took another grip and with a single mighty heave rolled the car body clear over. He gave me a knowing look and walked away without a word.

The Model T Ford was the automobile that put America on

wheels. It carried doctors through blizzards to attend the sick on lonely farms. Families went for Sunday drives, often as far as forty miles in a single day. The spirit of adventure was limitless. People travelled on roads thick with dust or thicker with mud, depending on the season of the year. They drove over blistering hot prairies, gravel mountain roads, cow paths, and wagon roads that ended in swamp. The old high-pressure 30x3½ tires were an endless source of trouble and frustration, but a broken-down Model T could often be repaired with nothing more than baling wire and bad language.

Driving one of those tin lizzies was high adventure. Service stations were often a hundred miles apart, so extra gas was carried in tins roped to the running boards. You carried food, water, and all the spare tires you could scrounge. It was great fun.

The Model T, in spite of all the jokes, was one of the world's great inventions. There can be no doubt about it. It started the travel era, and did more to open up the West than the Colt .45.

*AND
IN
CONCLUSION,
LADIES
AND
GENTLEMEN*

*I*n the preceding pages, I have attempted to portray the life and times of a generation which started school in 1920 or thereabouts, and were still young people at the outbreak of World War II in 1939.

Life was different then, though really no better nor worse than it is today. Most of our problems, worries, frustrations, were the same as those being experienced now, but with a few differences. Those differences are important. For instance, security was, to us, just another word in the dictionary. Company insurance plans and pensions were unknown except to those employed on the railroads or in enlightened enterprises. Labour unions were poorly organized and virtually powerless. A man could be discharged from his job at the whim of his employer. This happened with sickening frequency. There were logging companies on this coast which boasted of having three crews: one working, one leaving, and one arriving. Not that those leaving were any less efficient than those working or arriving. It was company policy to demonstrate unchallenged power over the work force.

Our schools were quite unlike modern ones. There are reactionaries today who deplore what they call "frills" in the modern educational system. Thinking back on my own experience of cold, draughty classrooms, uncomfortable desks, and an almost total absence of games of any kind, I am all for the "frills," even though they are not always appreciated by those whose privilege it is to have them.

Students in my day had to take out their frustrations and aggressions on someone, and fist fights were a daily occurrence. To give us credit, we fought fair—if fighting can ever be described as fair—with bare fists, never hitting below the belt. Kicking was frowned upon, and the karate chop had not made its debut.

Fighting was undoubtedly a natural reaction to iron discipline: whether the teacher was in the right or not, we did exactly as we were told or were severely punished. My hands and wrists were strapped until they bled. Such sadistic behaviour would not be tolerated now. In the third grade, we had a teacher whose notion of teaching spelling was to lay on the strap, one stroke per spelling error, after each Friday afternoon's ten-word test. To people like myself for whom the English language has never been a problem, her system was not too drastic for we made few mistakes. For students with a European or Asiatic background, life in Miss Oswald's class was a living horror. It is not easy to make a Japanese weep, but Miss Oswald could do it.

Looking on the bright side, we were not subjected to the awful pressures applied to today's young people. For job eligibility now, grade school education is worthless and high school, even university entrance, of little greater value. Employers are insisting more and more that a job applicant be a university graduate. In a few years no others will be considered. That is one kind of pressure. For those who must live and work in areas of high population density there is the unholy trinity of water, air, and noise pollution. The resulting tensions, the inability to relax, is another form of pressure. The realists find a sport or a hobby that takes them out of town as often as possible.

During that recession in our economy which has become known as the hungry thirties, city people did not fare too well. Nearly everyone knew periods of unemployment; many were on relief—as social assistance was then called—and even those who worked received such miserable wages that the future was bleak. By comparison, country folk had it made. They grew fine gardens, firewood was available in unlimited quantities, and game was plentiful. A man would share his deer with his neighbour, who in turn would present a salmon, a brace of grouse, or a sack of onions. Rural people, like pioneers of old, learned to depend upon each other rather than money. They dressed unstylishly, but ate well. Most important, they did not know the meaning of pressure.

We made our own amusements, my generation. At parties there was always someone who could play the piano or accordion, or even the lowly mouth organ.

It was much the same story with needed equipment. If we wanted a scooter, a wagon, or a rowboat, we made it ourselves or went without. We managed some ingenious applications of available material. When the propeller shaft stuffing box began to leak, repairs were often made with three short lengths of cotton rope soaked in bacon grease. I have frequently sandpapered a newly painted hull with dried dogfish skin. It may be slow work, but it imparts a fine finish. When one cannot afford fifteen cents for a tin of light machine oil, one must improvise. Ratfish liver, rendered down over low heat, produces a yellowish, almost odourless, high-quality oil excellent for guns and small machinery. If the old shotgun needed re-stocking or the military Lee-Enfield was to be converted into a sporting rifle, it was first necessary to search a woodpile—your own or your neighbour's—for a chunk of well-seasoned, straight-grained maple. Many hours of patient sawing and carving produced a fine stock, all the more appreciated because of the labour involved. We hand-made our own duck decoys, fishing rods, pack boards, and camping gear of all kinds. What is more, we enjoyed doing it. There is no peace of mind like that known to the individual craftsman.

Now that all that has been said, without rancour, you have a fair idea of our way of life. We had a fine time, and I would not have changed any of it. With the energetic adaptability and curiosity of youth, we did the best we could with what we had, and survived. The young are indestructible.